IPO YOUR SPAC !

The Step-by-Step Guide to finance
Your Special Purpose Acquisition Company
through an
Initial Public Offering
on
Wall Street

by Marc René DESCHENAUX

AUTHORED BY:
Marc René DESCHENAUX

PRINTED BY BOOKBABY
Printed in the United States of America
Available from The IPO Institute Website and retail outlets

First Printing Edition,2021
ISBN 978-1-7364515-9-5

PUBLISHED BY

SWISS FINANCIERS INNOVATIVE FINANCING TRADITION · IPO INSTITUTE · EXPERTS WITHOUT BORDERS THE ONLY PLACE TO FIND REAL EXPERTS · Greenberg, Hornblower, Deschenaux & Partners, LLP

DEDICATION

This book is dedicated to my daughters
Leila Deschenaux and Alia Deschenaux
as an expression of my infinite Love.

CONTENTS

Foreword

ABOUT THE AUTHOR

The detailed biography, achievements, press, videos, articles and other public information about Marc René DESCHENAUX can be found on the website https://Marc.Deschenaux.com.

Marc René DESCHENAUX is a Swiss jurist and a world-renowned expert in high finance.

He is the original founder of Greenberg Hornblower Deschenaux & Partners (GHD), an International Jurist Firm with headquarters in New York and offices in Los Angeles and with representative offices in Geneva Switzerland.

He is world widely regarded as the leading expert in Initial Public Offerings and a point of reference in securities, financing and trading law.

His expertise covers contract law, international corporate, governmental financing, bank syndication, non-profit law and global IP and securitization.

As an international financier, he is recognized for his state-of-the-art structures which have resulted in 179 successful IPOs and 243 private offerings – around two-thirds of these in private equity, and one-third in private debt.

He has organized several government loans, as well as the first national debt cancellation in history.

It is his negotiating skills and his background that set him apart from other lawyers. At the age of 15 years old he programmed a software (that was then used in a popular video game) for several hundred thousand dollars. Which he wisely used to self-finance his education.

He then founded several companies. Including Beat Perfumes, S.A., which created the Michael Jackson Perfume, and CD World Corporation. As

President and Founder of CD World, Marc René DESCHENAUX invented The MusicPoint™, a digital kiosk delivering a compact disc on demand.

Later, Marc René DESCHENAUX was chairman and founder of Investraders International Corporation, an investment bank in Geneva (Switzerland) specializing in distributing private offerings and organizing IPOs.

After graduating in law at the University in Geneva, he joined a traditional law firm Schwab Flaherty & Associés and then quickly struck out on his own as a jurist.

Having worked as a non-bar lawyer (also known as jurist) for more than a decade, he discovered a business model that permits Greenberg Hornblower Deschenaux & Partners to provide the legal services and Swiss Financiers to deliver financing services companies need but cannot obtain anywhere else.

Today, as "a man of action", he applies the lessons he has learned in a lifetime of entrepreneurship for the benefit of his clients.

One of these lessons is that litigation always represents a failure that could be avoided with proper counsel.

Another lesson is that without failure there can be no success.

Marc René DESCHENAUX is a native French speaker, and is able to carry out high level negotiations in English, German and Italian. He has knowledge of Spanish and Arabic. His Chinese is in progress.

EDUCATION: PhD candidate in law at the University of Geneva, Switzerland, master's degree in economic law, certification in transnational law, certification on the "Leading with Finance" course at Harvard Business School.

Mr Deschenaux was registered as a general securities representative (series 7) and general securities principal (series 24) by the North American Securities Dealers Association. He was a member of the National Investment Banking Association.

HONORS: Mr Deschenaux was elected to the Who's Who Legal Capital Markets in 2020 and as Man of the Year to the International Who's Who of Professionals (1999), and in 2003 he was invited by the United States Securities and Exchange Commission to speak at the 22nd Annual Government Business Forum on Small Business Capital Formation.

He was the treasurer, and a judge-mediator, at the International Court of Mediation and Arbitration (CIMEDA) from 2012 to 2020. He is now an Ambassador of the African Court of Mediation and Arbitration (CAMAR).

A WORD FROM HIS MENTOR

Marc René DESCHENAUX is the incarnation of the financial Genius.

Born from a single mother in the sixties, he was raised by his grand-father René DESCHENAUX a bank employee who has been president of both the Caisse Raiffeisen and of the insurance Chrétienne Sociale of Chêne-Bourg, a Geneva suburb, as well as of the ancient Geneva Stock Exchange, while working as a simple employee at Swiss Bank Corporation in the securities coupon department.

Marc René DESCHENAUX was doing interest rates calculations by age 7 and portfolio computations by age 9 on a mechanic calculator that did not feature multiplication and division functions!

Growing-up he received a Texas Instrument 59 calculator that taught him machine language, as one very special birthday gift from his grand-father. Marc worked hard doing little jobs and importing citizen band 27Mhz transmitters-receivers and talkie-walkies, to buy a second hand Commodore PET 2000 computer featuring a 6502 microprocessor, his true first microcomputer.

At age 11, he was sent to a catholic boarding school Collège Saint-Louis in Corsier Geneva for several years. He studied in Latin section. His grand-father died on the first day of his last year. Marc never recovered of his loss.

He developed software games and made enough money to pay for his own studies, first in electronics and data processing, in finance and financing, securities and commodities, futures and options, trading and pledging and finally in law and regulation.

His obsession for freedom in all sense of the words pushed him in studying finance, financing, complex corporate schemes, econometrics, leverage, equities, economics and attempting to mix quantum rules he always had a problem in understanding, to these various fields.

My purpose is not to write his detailed story, which would use another book, but to make the reader understand that at the time kids study letters and numbers, Marc was calculating financial portfolios for a rural saving & loan and at the time they were performing their first mathematical operations, he was programming computers in machine language. When his contemporaries were still at secondary school, he was a professional autodidact.

Later, in the middle of the eighties, two years before Jordan Belfort was hired by L.F. Rothschild as a securities representative for less than a month, let alone calling him the "Wolf of Wall Street", Marc's friends and colleagues called him "The Eagle of Wall Street".

This started as a joke because Marc was flying between New York and Geneva where he had his "nest" and because according to them, he was not really a Wall Street insider, but had more of a view from above on the market.

Over time, it became a mark of respect because of its extraordinarily accurate financial vision on the United States financial markets and creativity in legal strategy and schemes.

No wonder if today, he is the World Master of Experts in securities markets laws and regulations, finance, financings and econometrics.

He has been by far the most brilliant of my mentees and students.

Thomas J. MARCH

A WORD FROM HIS FIRST PARTNER

Marc Deschenaux deserves the praise of his teacher Tom March but as always, the best students go further than their masters. Marc has his own thoughts and actions which follow from his apprenticeship in IPOs.

It is often said to be an expert one needs to invest 10,000 hours before they can claim the title. Marc is an expert in so many things he must be nearly 100 years old. There are few people who have a grasp of how society and the economy work together, and it needs a person with multiple expertise's to behave within that understanding.

It is commonly agreed that Humanity has reached adulthood meaning we now are responsible for ourselves and our planet. Marc intuitively knows this and understands the engine of society is the economy, but he goes further behaving as the engine is the wrong metaphor as society, the economy and all other aspects of the planet are alive.

In a new way of looking at the economy the institutions and processes are not just in need of renewal they are in need of constant change as are all living things.

Marc describes the current IPO institutions and processes in a way we can understand in the old mode. However, with careful reading he is suggesting a movement into a new mode.

In the economy as it is there are other deep-seated issues among them are the fundaments of dealing with Intellectual property and knowledge of the space as a whole.

If you review his CV, you will note he has actions in both of these areas.

Marc is beginning to show his many areas of expertise and we hope his first book will be a success in showing that IPOs are the way to make sure new knowledge is brought to the benefit of society.

There must surely be further gems from this fertile mind.

Mike Horner Founder of Company X,
First Partner of Deschenaux & Partners,
Precious Advisor & Mentor to Marc Deschenaux

Introduction

A special purpose acquisition company (SPAC) is a company with no commercial operations that is formed strictly to raise capital through an Initial Public Offering (IPO) for the purpose of acquiring another existing company. [1]

Designed to take companies public without going through the traditional IPO process. SPACs allow retail investors to invest in private equity type transactions, particularly leveraged buyouts.

According to the U.S. Securities and Exchange Commission (SEC), "A SPAC is created specifically to pool funds in order to finance a merger or acquisition opportunity within a set timeframe. The opportunity usually has yet to be identified."[2]

Also known as "blank check companies", SPACs have been around for decades. In recent years, they've become more popular, attracting big-name underwriters and investors and raising a record amount of IPO money.[1]

---

[1] (Investopedia, 2020)
[2] (Wikipedia, 2020)

The Typical SPAC Scenario

A SPAC raises capital through an Initial Public Offering (IPO) for the purpose of acquiring an existing operating company.

The sponsor, typically a person or team with significant business experience, decides to launch a SPAC.

They create a holding company.

The sponsor also receives 20% of the shares of the SPAC as a fee, called a "promote" or "founders shares."

A SPAC raises capital through an Initial Public Offering (IPO) for the purpose of acquiring an existing operating company.

Then the sponsor complete the normal filings associated with going public through an IPO.

At the time of their IPOs, SPACs have no existing business operations or even stated targets for acquisition.

Because the company doesn't do anything (i.e. it has no operational business), the filing process is fast and easy.

The sponsor then goes on a roadshow, similar to traditional IPOs, to try to find interested investors.

Investors in SPACs can range from well-known institutional investors to private investment funds.

The difference here is that they are selling themselves, their team, their vision and their experience, rather than a specific company.

Once the sponsor has attracted enough interest, they sell securities in the company.

The money raised from the IPO is put into a blind trust, and is untouchable until the shareholders approve the acquisition transaction.

The SPAC goes public and trades on an exchange like any other publicly traded company.

This is where the general public gets involved. They can purchase securities on the open market, but the future acquisition is still unknown to them.

Instead, these investors are buying on the vision and the strength of the sponsor or the promise of a strong future acquisition.

Once the SPAC is public, the sponsors can begin the hunt for a target company to acquire.

Target Type

There are no restrictions on the type of company a SPAC can acquire, though many will highlight a target industry before IPO. Subsequently, an operating company can merge with, or be acquired by, the publicly traded SPAC and become a listed company in lieu of executing its own IPO.[3]

When the sponsors find a company, they then negotiate the terms of the acquisition with the target company, like purchase price or company valuation.

Following a deal, the "de-SPAC" process begins..

---

[3] (pwc Price Waterhouse Cooper, 2017)

de-SPAC

After deciding on the terms of the acquisition or of the merger, the sponsors must propose the acquisition target to shareholders.

VOTE

The shareholders have the opportunity to vote on the contemplated transaction whether acquisition or merger, which gives them some recourse if a sponsor chooses a company they do not like.

Even if the acquisition is approved, shareholders can then redeem their shares for their money back.

No Satisfying Target Found Case

Typically, the sponsors have 2 years to find and announce a transaction whether acquisition or merger, or else the SPAC will dissolve and shareholders will get their money back. SPACs have two years to complete a transaction or they must return their funds to investors.[4]

Investors in SPACs can range from well-known institutional investors to the general public.

Subsequently, an operating company can merge with, or be acquired by, the publicly traded SPAC and become a listed company in lieu of executing its own IPO.[5]

Merger Case

Proceeds are put in a trust account after the IPO and the SPAC normally has 18-24 months to find and execute a merger with a target firm[6].

---

[4] (Investopedia, 2020)
[5] (pwc Price Waterhouse Cooper, 2017)
[6] (pwc Price Waterhouse Cooper, 2017)

Acquisition Case

.

SPACs have two years to complete an acquisition or they must return their funds to investors.[7]

The purpose of this book is to provide you with a step-by-step guide to finance your special purpose acquisition company through an initial public offering (IPO) on Wall Street.

[7] (Investopedia, 2020)

IPO YOUR SPAC !

CHAPTER 1

Chapter 1: SPAC Definition

Special Purpose Acquisition Company

Investopedia defines Special Purpose Acquisition Company (SPAC) as a "non-trading company created solely to raise capital through an initial public offering (IPO) for the purpose of purchasing an established company. (Investopedia, 2020)

The Securities & Exchange Commission defines it as a type of blank check company. SPACs have become a popular vehicle for various transactions, including transitioning a company from a private company to a publicly traded company. Certain market participants believe that, through a SPAC transaction, a private company can become a publicly traded company with more certainty as to pricing and control over deal terms as compared to traditional initial public offerings, or IPOs.

These types of transactions, most commonly where a SPAC acquires or merges with a private company, occur after, often many months or more than a year after, the SPAC has completed its own IPO. Unlike an operating company that becomes public through a traditional IPO, however, a SPAC is a shell company when it becomes public. This means that it does not have an underlying operating business and does not have assets other than cash and limited investments, including the proceeds from the IPO.

Blank Check Company

A blank check company is a development stage company that has no specific business plan or purpose or has indicated its business plan is to engage in a merger or acquisition with an unidentified company or companies, other entity, or person. These companies typically involve speculative investments and often fall within the SEC's definition of "penny stocks" or are considered "microcap stocks."

In addition, a blank check company registering for a securities offering may be subject to additional requirements for the protection of investors, including depositing most of the raised funds in an escrow account until an acquisition is agreed to and requiring shareholder approval of any identified acquisition.

A type of Blank Check Company is a "special purpose acquisition company" or SPAC for short. A SPAC is created specifically to pool funds in order to finance a merger or acquisition opportunity within a set timeframe. The opportunity usually has yet to be identified.

SPACs are non-operating publicly listed entities, established to find and acquire a private company, activating the publicly listed stock of the acquisition target.

SPACs are also referred to as blank check businesses. It is considered a reverse merger whenever a SPAC or other publicly-traded corporation buys a private company. A merger typically occurs when a private corporation makes a public company private.

In 2020, 247 newly created SPACs generated $83 billion in capital via initial public offerings, as per SPAC Insider. More SPACs were established in 2019 and 2020 than in the previous 18 years together. (Insider, 2020).

Not only is the quantity of SPACs growing, but each SPAC raises enough capital via IPOs to be able to buy larger private firms.

Compared with $230 million in 2019, the average SPAC IPO in 2020 was $336 million.

The Difference between a SPAC and an IPO

The typical IPO process is turned on its head by a SPAC in that the business that originally goes public is not so much a corporation as the expectation of one. In other words, the SPAC is just a shell company that does not own any assets itself.

Investopedia defines a Shell company as "an organization without actual business activities or substantial assets. (Kenton, 2020)

A SPAC can be seen as the opposite of a conventional IPO. A SPAC first goes public, typically with a highly respected management team capable of raising capital from large institutional investors, with the goal of purchasing a private firm within around 24 months to place it in its shell.

An IPO is essentially a money-seeking business, whereas a SPAC is a business seeking money. Going public via a SPAC will speed up the market entry of a business by anywhere from two to four months.

Considering the lack of financial reports and related materials, there are fewer SEC concerns and queries to answer without a corporation in the actual shell, which shortens the auditing process.

Additionally, instead of attempting to sell a business to public investors at a roadshow, a SPAC provides added assurity of getting a long-term investor base through a private-public equity fund, or PIPE, that is in place.

Usually, that kind of assurance is not available in an IPO unless it is perfectly clear that the business will do well.

Why Does a SPAC Exist?

One of the first questions that people ask about SPACs is why do they exist in the first place?

One of the foremost reasons SPACs exist is that private firms are ready to be acquired by them as it is more convenient and less cumbersome than going public with an initial public offering (IPO).

Based on the economic circumstances and the risk appetite of investors, the responsiveness of the capital markets to new public offerings can vary.

Since a SPAC is already public, a reverse merger enables a private corporation to become public when the IPO window is shut.

SPAC acquisitions are also appealing to private corporations because their investors and other key shareholders will sell a larger proportion of their ownership in a reverse takeover than they would in an IPO.

The founders of private companies may also bypass the lock-up periods needed for initial public offerings to sell new public stock with SPAC.

However, the main question that needs to be answered is why you should opt for a SPAC and not an IPO?

Well, because an IPO can be hard work and there's no guaranteed success at the end of it all.

Firstly, you have the roadshow, where you attempt to get investors involved, and until fairly close to the sale, there's confusion about the valuation.

You also negotiate with different investors, typically institutional investors, which is confusing and frustrating. Additionally, your IPO can be tanked by uncertainty. A classic example of this is WeWork.

The corporation was hoping to raise about $4 billion in an IPO. Instead, people produced humorous interpretations of their S-1 as a comedy routine, and the IPO was cancelled. (Eavis & Meced, 2019)

To add to the above, there seems to be more confusion now than in the previous years. The Covid-19 pandemic has rendered the markets a little crazier than normal.

If I'm operating a unicorn and I have to generate funds, the IPO might not look as good as it used to once. Perhaps I want something that's simpler or less risky.

The IPO is already completed with SPAC. All you need to do is negotiate with a party: the SPAC that will acquire you.

That implies that you were already aware of the valuation, there's no need to conduct a roadshow, and you can out your current investors. Moreover, since you are negotiating with just one party, the entire process is much quicker.

Lastly, the pitch is really easy when you compare it to an IPO. In short, SPAC is a better way of going public than a typical IPO under the current climate

So, how does a Special Purpose Acquisition Company (SPAC) work? The details of this are provided next.

How Do SPACs Work?

SPACs generate funds to make an acquisition via an IPO. A conventional SPAC IPO arrangement comprises a common share of Class A stock paired with a warrant. A warrant provides the holder with the right to purchase more stock at a set price later.

Investors who take part in the SPAC IPO are drawn by the ability to exercise the warrants so that, once the purchase target is determined and the deal concludes, they can get more common stock shares. The following are the most important things to know about SPACs.

FOUNDERS

Seasoned business executives create a special purpose acquisition company (SPAC); they are optimistic that their credibility and expertise can help them find a successful company to acquire.

Since SPAC is just a shell company, the founders become the selling point when raising money from investors.

The founders provide the business with the starting capital, and they profit from a significant stake in the acquired firm.

When establishing a special purpose acquisition business, the founders typically have an interest in a particular industry.

IPO Issuance

When launching the IPO, the SPAC management team hires an investment firm to administer the IPO.

The investment bank and the corporation's management team decide on a fee to be paid for the service, generally around 10% of the IPO revenue.

Securities issued during an IPO are provided at a price per unit, representing one or more common stock shares.

As the SPAC does not have any performance records or revenue data, the SPAC prospectus emphasizes primarily on the sponsors rather than on business history and revenues.

All funds from the IPO are kept in a trust account till a private firm is established as an acquisition target.

Target Company Acquisition

The management team has 18–24 months to select a target and conclude the acquisition after SPAC has generated the capital needed via an IPO.

Depending on the firm and business, the duration can vary. However, the target firm's fair market value must be 80 percent or more of the trust assets of the SPAC. (Harroch, Raman, & Vanderlaan, 2020)

When the acquisition is complete, the founders will take advantage of their shareholding in the new company, typically 20% of the common stock, while the shareholders will receive equity interest on the basis of their capital investment.

In the case that the agreed period expires before the completion of the acquisition, the SPAC is terminated and the income from the IPO held in the trust account is returned to the shareholders.

The management team is not supposed to earn salaries while running the SPAC until the contract is concluded.

SPAC Capital Structure

The following are the key components that make the capital structure of a SPAC.

Public Units

To conclude the acquisition of a private business, a SPAC floats an IPO to collect the necessary money

The funding is generated through retail and institutional investors and 100 percent of the money generated in the IPO is kept in a trust account

In exchange for their investment, shareholders are provided with units, with each unit containing a portion of common stock and, at a later date, a warrant to buy more stock.

The selling price of the shares per unit is normally $10.00. After the IPO, the units are divided into common stock shares and warrants that can be sold publicly

The intent behind the warrant is to provide extra compensation to shareholders for making investments in SPAC.

Founder Shares

At the beginning of the SPAC filing, the founders of the SPAC will receive founder shares and pay minimal compensation for the number of shares, resulting in a 20 percent interest in the outstanding shares following the completion of the IPO.

The shares are meant to pay the management team, who are not entitled to receive any compensation or fee from the company after the conclusion of an acquisition process.

What are Warrants in SPACs and How Do They Work?

We briefly mentioned warrants above, but what are they specifically and how do they work?

A portion of a warrant is present in the units issued to the public, allowing investors to buy an entire share of the common stock.

One warrant may be excised for a portion of a share (either half, one-third or two-thirds) or a whole share of the stock, depending on the SPAC's size and the bank issuing the IPO.

For instance, the warrant could be exercisable at $16.50 per share if the unit price in the IPO is $15.

The warrants become exercisable either thirty days after the De-SPAC transaction or an entire year following the SPAC IPO.

The public warrants are cash-settled, which ensures that to obtain a full share of stock, the investor would have to pay the full price of the warrant in cash.

On the other hand, Founder warrants could be net settled, which ensures that they are not expected to offer cash to obtain a full share of stock

Instead, stock shares with a fair market value proportional to the difference between the stock exchange price and the strike price of a warrant are issued to them.

Are SPACs New?

Not at all. SPACs were quite common about forty years ago but developed a negative reputation when some individuals used them to scam investors and fill their own pockets.

Money was almost always lost by investors, and [SPACs] disappeared from view.

However, SPACs have now made a worthy comeback. While not a new solution, the SPAC IPO path has increased tremendously in popularity over the previous year.

There were 248 SPAC IPOs in 2020. This is thrice the number of SPAC IPOs compared to any single year before this.

Why Are SPACs Growing in Popularity?

In the mid-2010s, SPACs proceeded on their suddenly respectable path. Some of the people who became involved include mutual fund firms like Rowe Price and Fidelity and T, investment banks like Goldman Sachs, Credit Suisse, and Morgan Stanley, as well as celebrities, hedge fund managers, and big-name founders like Michael Jordan, Bill Ackerman, and Richard Branson.

In 2020, their numbers have soared. As per SPAC Research, which collects data on SPACs, SPACs launched 128 IPOs at the beginning of October 2020, generating a total of $49.1 billion. (Daks, 2020)

This a lot higher than 2019, when a maximum of $ 13.6 billion was generated by just 59 SPACs.

The Coronavirus pandemic has definitely been a factor. Because of how they operate, SPACs tend to do better in times of stock market downturn.

Additionally, SPACs offer several benefits not provided by a conventional IPO to sponsor-organizers and businesses that choose to go public. One is the simplified criteria for disclosure that saves trees, funds, and time.

Another possible reason is that in recent years, there have been instances of businesses such as WeWork taking the conventional IPO route and decreasing in value during the roadshow phase due to investor scrutiny, causing the company to withdraw its IPO filing.

By contrast, the SPAC IPO path entails relatively less investor scrutiny because the entity going public is not really a corporation, so there is not much to scrutinize.

This renders the SPAC IPO more appealing to riskier businesses or businesses in riskier sectors, such as the media industry.

This is particularly true if the current investors in those firms are anxious and looking for the business to sell or go public in order to cash out their shares.

Firms that are "risky enough" that they might not be accepted in the normal IPO market are those that are likely to opt for a SPAC IPO.

In a SPAC IPO, however, the scrutiny is not actually abolished. Instead, it is redirected and reduced.

The initial investors make the call of whether to take a gamble on the sponsor and acquisition strategy of the SPAC, knowing that if a majority disagrees with the ultimate acquisition target, they will have their money refunded.

Therefore, the acquisition could be more scrutinized by investors than the IPO. On the other hand, they (the investors) have already endorsed the sponsor championing the acquisition.

Therefore, the investors are likely to go along with the transaction unless the sponsor really goes off track with the acquisition target.

The involvement of fewer individuals is another reason SPAC IPOs are so popular.

A conventional IPO involves many investors negotiating concurrently with issuers and underwriters on particular terms such as underwriter rights, executive pay, the offer price, and several other issues.

However, in a SPAC, it is generally just the target company and the sponsor that are involved in the negotiations. This helps to speed up the process.

Can Any Company Become Public Via a SPAC?

This is a difficult one to answer. There seem to be no laws stopping a corporation from developing its own SPAC and then getting the SPAC to acquire it. However, this is not what happens in reality.

Rather, after the SPAC has gone public and the money for the purchase has been generated, the SPAC sponsor goes about seeking a business to acquire.

In addition, SPACs are not allowed to have a merger target in mind when they go public.

Advantages of a SPAC

Selling to a SPAC may be a promising prospect for smaller business owners; these businesses are mostly private equity firms.

Firstly, relative to a traditional private equity offer, selling to a SPAC will add up to 20 percent to the sale price.

Additionally, under the guidance of an established partner, being acquired by a SPAC may also provide business owners with what is basically a quicker IPO operation, with less concern about the fluctuations in wider market sentiment.

However, the advantages of a SPAC are not limited to these. Instead, there are many more advantages of a SPAC to consider, and we will go through each of them next.

Chapter 2: SPAC Advantages of a SPAC

As of the first week of October 2020, SPAC IPOs had surpassed 135 new listings in 2020, generating total revenue of over $50 billion, as per SPACInsider.com. (Insider, 2020)

In July of that year, when Bill Ackman and Pershing Square collected $4 billion, one of the most prominent SPACs was finalized, becoming the biggest SPAC on record.

Compared to 2019, the overall proceeds, with two and half months still remaining in the year, had risen more than four times.

The growing popularity of SPACs is due to the many advantages that they offer. In most cases, the benefits of a SPAC far exceed the potential risks.

Additionally, the characteristics of these types of investment vehicles include reverse merger transaction prospects for investors and target companies that exceed their typical reverse merger counterparts.

If you intend to use a SPAC to prevent Rule 419 that forbids trading, you must not be a penny stock.

This means that you must generate at least $5,000,000 net of all fees and expenditures, including those charged as permitted to the promoters. You must also show more than a $5 trading price, which includes an underwritten offering in almost all instances.

By ensuring the above, you will open yourself up to the many advantages that are offered by a SPAC.

Despite entering the mainstream, SPACs are not completely understood outside the investment community.

However, this does take away from the fact that SPACs today offer an effective alternative to the conventional IPO and a viable alternative to private equity firms that usually search for an exit after a couple of years.

The following are some of the main advantages of going public via a SPAC instead of the traditional IPO or direct listing route.

Time Advantages

A SPAC's most significant benefit is the time it takes between planning to go public and actually becoming a publicly traded company.

The executive team of an organization does not want to spend 12 to 18 months corresponding with the underwriters and the SEC followed by a pre-IPO roadshow.

SPACs provide businesses with an opportunity to go public in just 4-6 months, allowing additional time for the team to concentrate on developing the company and growing shareholder value.

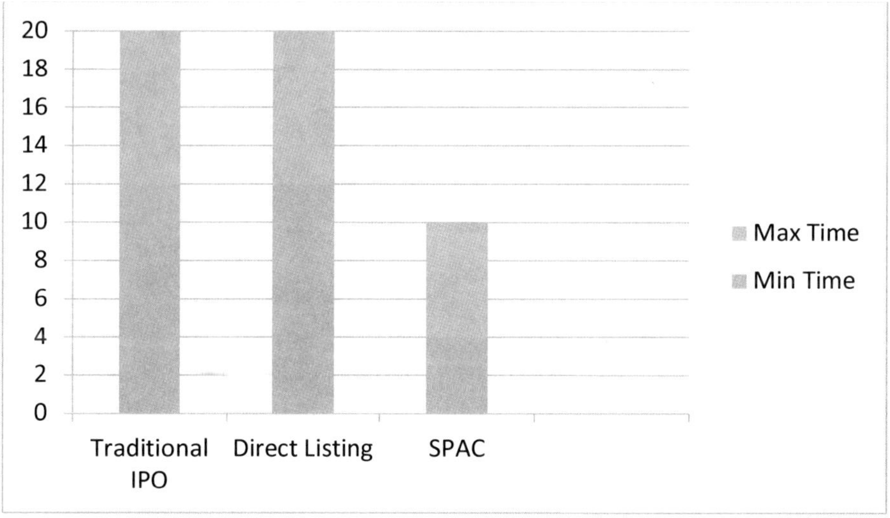

Since the IPO process can be abstracted by SPACs, a private firm can merge into an already publicly traded (blank shell) corporation with substantially less work than expected for a conventional IPO.

For the SPAC IPO, SEC registration documents are brief and can be completed within a few weeks. Historical financial reports or properties that need to be disclosed are not needed.

In addition, the SPAC sponsors spend the coming months on roadshows to generate money.

SPACs assume all IPO activity on the boilerplate, allowing the target organization to discuss just conditions, terms, and other regular M&A processes.

Not only is merging with a SPAC a faster way to go public than direct listing or a traditional IPO, but it also relieves you from the responsibilities of a roadshow.

This is because a roadshow is not a requirement with a SPAC. There's no need to sell yourself and gain the attention of investors.

This is great news considering travel, in-person meetings, activities, and other discussions are more regulated and can introduce new risks.

Therefore, acquiring a SPAC is a saner operation that generates less urgent and prolonged scrutiny.

And since a roadshow is not required, the SPAC will spend more time concentrating on priorities such as your business, providing greater emphasis and reducing the time needed to obtain access to public markets.

No 'IPO Window' Advantages

Timing is the most important thing in a conventional IPO and missing the appropriate "window" may be the difference between a good "pop" and a poor IPO-at least by certain standards.

On the other hand, the very concept of a SPAC fits well with the somewhat shut IPO window.

The SPAC market is mostly active and could be even more so when economic uncertainty or macro shocks shut the IPO window.

The risks of not raising the capital via institutional investors or adjusting the price of the offer are all avoided as these are accomplished when the money for the SPAC is generated and put in the investment fund for holding. This has been done many times already.

Cost Advantages

While expenses for a SPAC do not differ too much from expenditures for a conventional IPO, the arrangement of discounts for underwriters and the overall subscription process can be more advantageous for a business looking to go public.

One or more investment banks that earn an underwriting concession as an incentive to promote and sell the IPO can be underwriters of a conventional IPO.

The discount for conventional IPO underwriters is generally about 3.5-7 percent, as per PWC. (pwc)

On the other hand, the SPAC IPO's underwriting concession is 5.5%, with 2% payment during the IPO and the remainder 3.5% payment at the time of the de-SPAC transaction. (Levine, 2020)

In addition, the underwriting discount payment is usually made as equity options in the business to the SPAC sponsors.

The delayed discount commission helps the target organization and positively influences sponsors to identify a target acquisition to earn their 3.5 percent commission as equity.

To say it another way, instead of paying the SPAC sponsors in the form of equity, the payment that a corporation would make to an investment bank to underwrite an IPO is instead made to the SPAC sponsors.

Although the cost of going public could be more or less the same, in comparison to a conventional IPO, benefits for underwriters and the business are more integrated in the SPAC process.

Knowledge Management

As a key advisor in a SPAC merger, the management team will always retain at least one key individual for an active role within the corporation or on the board.

After any key transaction is finalized, this helps mitigate the possibility of the company struggling to achieve investor goals.

Availability of Cash

SPACs usually have cash, unlike the majority of non-operational shell companies.

In most situations, the cash would be less than $5 million in a standard SPAC, but the money is helpful in generating instant capital appreciation and valuation for the transaction target.

No IPO Threshold

In the conventional sense, since many smaller businesses do not qualify for an IPO, a SPAC is a good option for businesses that do not make the cut but that may still have significant potential growth opportunities.

No History to Worry About

There is no controversy, expense and hassle of cleaning a former shell company because SPACs lack the questionable past of many previously reporting firms in a reverse merger transaction.

No Unexpected Liabilities

Since the SPAC has not carried out any material activity and has a clean balance sheet, the target company's shareholders usually face no unforeseen liabilities after the transaction concludes.

Flexible Ownership and Control

SPACs do not need to take care of the target or to supplant current management.

For instance, we have seen SPAC transactions varying from a 100 percent purchase of the target business to SPAC investors stepping in as a partner to supply the current management/ownership with partial liquidity and/or growth capital.

Capital Source Advantages

Without debt service expenses, amortization and agreements intrinsic to debt capital, SPACs can provide equity capital for investment. or development.

Additionally, they can provide permanent capital, enabling management to concentrate on generating long-term value instead of the short-term growth that is often required to satisfy the return barriers that private equity firms require.

Pricing and Valuation Advantages

SPACs offer the sponsors (underwriters) a stronger incentive structure for the target business to collect capital on favorable terms.

Investment banks that underwrite the conventional IPO do not have the same motivations as the business. Banks want to retain their sales relationships and sell shares in firms that are likely to make the most money for their clients.

Examples of the mismatch of rewards between banks and the long-term performance of a pre-IPO business are Greenshoe options and over-allotment options.

It is not unusual for a corporation's stocks, also known as "pop," to trade higher than the IPO price when they're first listed on an exchange.

Banks ignore the corporation's concerns and inappropriately price the IPO to make a pop to reward early investors (clients of the bank) who assume more risk.

A big pop encourages banks to sell more shares to stabilize the price, a mechanism referred to as over-allotment. In this case, because they have earned capital at a much lower valuation, the business leaves money on the table.

On the other hand, when there is no pop and the stock trades slightly lower than the IPO price, the option for underwriters to buy back shares is provided by a lack of supply to push the price back up.

This is the greenshoe alternative, which is typically written during the phase of underwriting.

The above options allow banks to monitor the IPO process to minimize drawbacks for themselves and their clients.

As the sponsors are basically the underwriters of a SPAC, they ultimately have the same long-term benefits as the corporation. It can be viewed as an M&A approach rather than a transaction.

While discussions can be complicated, they're all on the same page until the merger is accomplished.

In addition, when they are positive about a target firm, sponsors of the SPAC place their credibility on the line. This generally results in the firm's fair and favorable valuation.

Advantages for Investors

Till now, we have looked at the benefits of a SPAC from the perspective of the target company. However, it is also important to consider the advantages of a SPAC from an investor's perspective.

This is required to understand whether going public via a SPAC from an investment viewpoint is a feasible option or not. This understanding can be reached by going through the following investor advantages of a SPAC.

Tradable Stocks & Warrants

During and after the interim period, investors in SPACs are permitted to trade both their warrants and stock while they search for a good target firm to merge-in.

Usually, the stock in such a possible reverse merger deal with a SPAC would drop slightly because costs incurred in the SPAC development phase would have depleted the shell capital.

However, a shareholder can effectively sell their stock from the time the SPAC is produced and anywhere afterward.

When an agreement is signed, the stock will always tick back to value before the announcement of the merger.

In the case of an upside in the transaction, such an investor may sell their shares, prevent the loss by selling them at cost and then retain holdings in the warrants, which could also theoretically yield good returns. It could be a win-win-win-win.

Funds in Escrow

Because the entire lump sum of investors is automatically put in escrow (and receives a small amount of interest when awaiting a merger), the downside risk is substantially reduced.

In the worst possible case, an offer never materializes. The shareholder fails to get a 5% to 10% return on the market and instead gets a few points over zero.

Nevertheless, the risk seems to be well worth it for the future upside probability when a good merger applicant comes along, provided the downside is reasonably covered.

Greater Input

A SPAC allows for greater investor involvement in the transactions themselves, unlike a venture capital pool where few investors join in and invest their funds in a 'blind pool' to be managed exclusively by the VC fund management team.

SPAC shareholders do not pick the deals, but they can pull out of any target opportunity and obtain funding reimbursement.

Additionally, any prospect identified as a target in the reverse merger transaction can be voted on by an investor.

In short, maybe the biggest benefit in a SPAC transaction from an investor's point of view is the opportunity to have a say (yes/no) in the investment decision-a function that varies significantly from the venture capital world's blind pools.

Time Limitation Incentives

There is never an open-ended time allocation to finalize a deal in SPAC situations.

There is often a cap that pushes the SPAC team to find a target within a given time span (say two years).

Although there is still lock-up and illiquidity for a period of time before the merger takes place, it is still minimal. It guarantees investors can be confident that if an agreement between investors and management is never settled upon, then the original funds are returned.

Working with a SPAC often ensures that the target company retains many of the privileges of self-filing, albeit without the advantage of a capital raising activity.

Additionally, a SPAC agreement is usually easier than self-filing and typically comes with more seasoned managers and business experts to help the deal succeed eventually.

While SPAC has many advantages, there is also a range of SPAC risks that must be considered, especially for corporations that want to merge with a blank-check company in order to go public or access capital. The disadvantages or risks of a SPAC are what we will be looking at next.

Chapter 3: SPAC Disadvantages

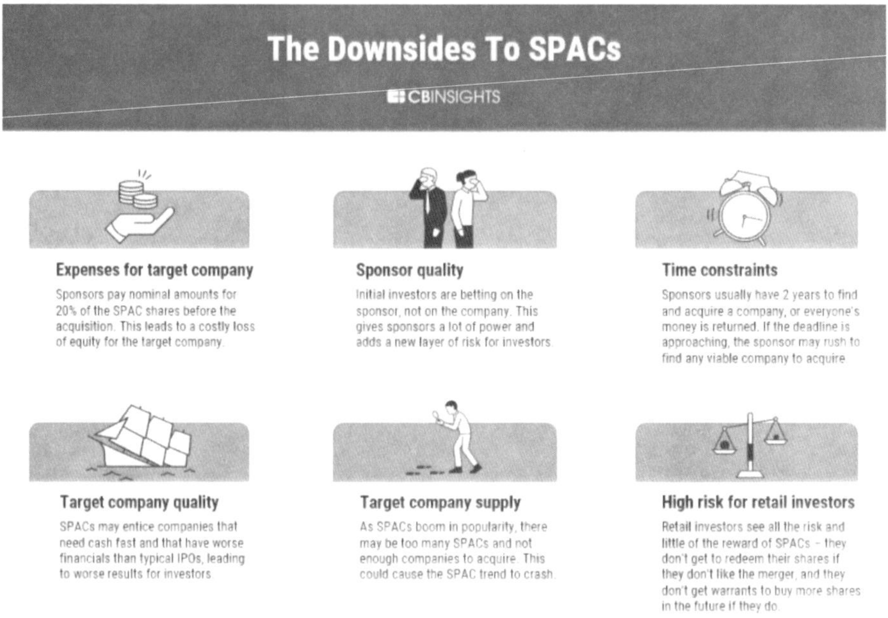

There are some specific costs and risks that must be properly considered, alongside the unique advantages that result from a SPAC transaction

For instance, at the time of the initial business merger, SPAC investors have the option to recover their equity if they do not wish to retain their holding through the merger.

Suppose the sponsor is not able to draw new investors to cover the funding. In that case, the redemptions will reduce the capital available for the deal and render the transaction infeasible if a reasonable amount of money cannot be substituted.

Therefore, the possibilities represented by SPACs come with a range of problems that private sector officers and directors need to seriously think about.

Most critically, businesses need to get to know the team that constitutes a sponsor of SPAC. Look for abilities and characteristics that are complementary to the company's needs.

In particular, the acquired business should be assisted by people with comprehensive capital markets, management and board expertise as it tries to adapt to the public markets.

In addition, an experienced team of sponsors will provide management with strategic and organizational support, helping to plug gaps and expand talent across the company.

When they sell to those who specialize in the business field of the target organization, management is more likely to gain much needed support from sponsors.

Expertise in finding trapped value in businesses and helping to develop plans that will fully realize that value comes is ensured with industry specialization.

While SPACs are not expected to follow an industry strategy, most of them are involved in a single or restricted number of sectors.

A key concern is the extent to which sponsors exert power. SPACs pursuing 100% equity in the target business cannot be suitable long-term partners. And this is just one risk or disadvantage associated with a SPAC. There are many more that also need to be considered.

The following are the risks or disadvantages of a SPAC that must be considered before a final decision on going public via a SPAC is made.

Valuation Risk

In a SPAC merger, the evaluation of the target firm is subject to negotiation.

However, since the approval of the SPAC shareholders is required for the merger and SPAC shareholders can choose to redeem their stake in the company, the valuation must be considered by such shareholders as acceptable, or the transaction may result in higher redemptions and thus less operating capital for the go-forward business.

Also, you might not get long-term investors apart from the sponsor. This is because people who invest in SPACs have different objectives than a regular investor.

For instance, they may not know or care about your business until it's time to acquire it.

Some investors may also be cautious about purchasing shares in a business that went public via a SPAC.

This is because the level of due diligence needed for a merger may be lower than what a standard IPO requires, as mandated by the Securities and Exchange Commission. This may make investors skeptical about a company that went public via a SPAC.

More Expensive Than IPOs

SPAC IPOs are typically more expensive than a conventional IPO. This is because you generally need to make payments to investment banks between 1 and 7% of what you generated to conduct an IPO.

The underwriter receives 5.5 percent in a SPAC and other expenses may be involved in the merger. For example, you must pay a bank to get advice on the deal.

So SPAC expenses are about a quarter of the funds collected – three or four times greater than what you would pay in an IPO. Additionally, in most instances, 20 percent of the stock is given 'on the cheap' to the sponsor.

Accounting and Finance Gap

As an existing business, you'll already have created functions such as finance and accounting. However, since a SPAC is a shell corporation with no activities, these teams do not have in-house teams.

For example, most would involve third-party partners to perform these functions. Therefore, between the capacities of your company and the SPAC, there will often be some discrepancy.

In addition, the internal teams do not have the skills required to follow the steps, the nuanced criteria for documentation, or other strategic factors specific to a SPAC being acquired.

Target firms have often disregarded the finance and technical accounting functions needed to manage these transactions.

And several of them may also be unprepared to undertake the comprehensive due diligence procedure that can again divert managers from day-to-day tasks while exposing businesses to unexpected threats if they are not carefully investigated.

Non Approval of Deal after Investment of Time, Money, and Effort

The target company risks losing a great deal of time, money, and legal fees invested in working on a deal with a SPAC if the SPAC investors do not accept it.

In this case, the associated PIPE funding cannot be raised or, more typically, the SPAC investors may redeem a large portion of the funds in the trust account.

A Suitable Target Firm May Not Be Found Within the Required Timeframe

Over the prescribed time span (usually two years, with certain extensions of up to 18 months or 3 years), the SPAC may not find an appropriate merger, and investor money would be tied up for that duration.

In the low-interest-rate setting we are presently in, the lost opportunity cost of the resources being tied up has been lowered.

Investors are usually seen to be paid by both the warrants for this opportunity cost and by obtaining optionality on the De-SPAC deal if the stock price trades up on launch.

In any case, the organization looking to go public via a SPAC would be at a loss if a suitable target firm isn't found within the specified timeframe.

Plenty of Paperwork

If you are searching for a strategic partner but don't want to manage the troubles and time commitments of a conventional IPO, being bought by or merging with a SPAC is a great option.

That said, it is essential to recognize that an S-4, which contains the specifics of a merger or acquisition, would still have to be filed with the U.S. Commission for Securities and Exchange (SEC).

Many of the specifications, such as filing an S-1 to list the securities with the SEC, are identical to a typical IPO as well.

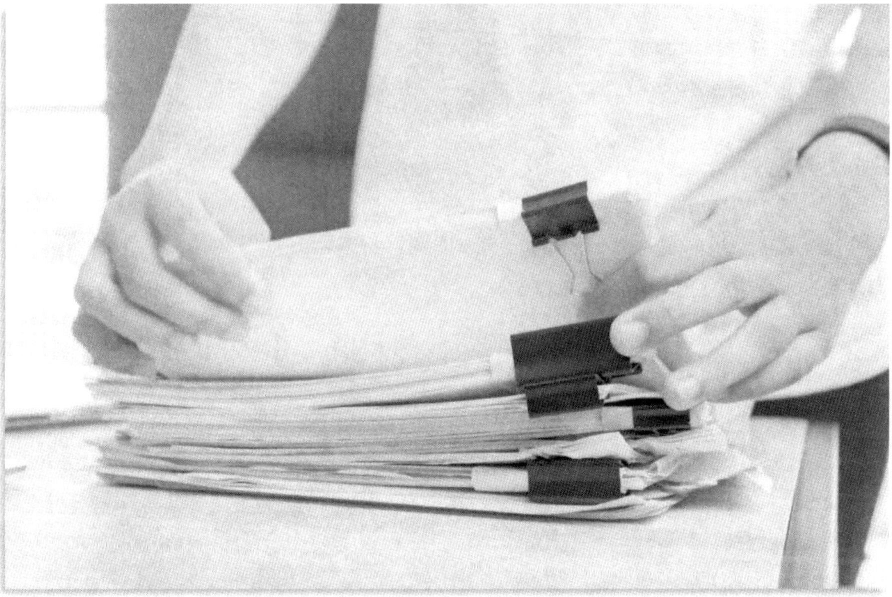

If the appropriate paperwork is not completed or improperly submitted, businesses may experience regulatory snags that stall the transaction and distract managers from key business efforts.

Additionally, due to the lack of sufficient internal controls or SEC-mandated financial reports, a target company could simply not be ready for a public company.

In consultation with the target business auditors, this is a crucial problem to be rooted out early on.

A Closed Deal Isn't Necessarily a 'Successful' Deal

There may be further SPAC risks that arise following a closed deal, depending on your business. For instance, in the sense that a sale to SPAC would not indicate a "complete" exit, there are unique considerations for private equity-backed businesses.

As investors look to optimize their returns by secondary sales after the merger, this may cause some nuance.

In order to help both parties understand their choices and maximize results for those concerned, a third party may also play a valuable role.

In addition, if the transaction takes the business into new markets or needs other big changes, refining procedures would help you move forward quickly and efficiently.

This is especially true at a time when previously private corporations are adjusting to the oversight that is part of the requirements for disclosure for public companies.

Sponsor Quality

Initial investors are betting on the sponsor rather than the company. This gives sponsors a lot of power and adds a new layer of risk for sponsors.

All other investors will face immediate dilution after the business merger concludes because of the standard 20 percent of founding shares granted to SPAC sponsors.

However, while the sponsors receive 20 percent ownership in the SPAC, this share cannot be used to redeem cash held in trust.

This implies that if the sponsor fails to close a deal, their equity stake will become pointless.

Therefore, management must assess the potential effect of sponsor warrants, investor warrants, and any private placement while considering the cost of capital compared to other funding sources in order to derive the completely diluted effects of the merger on their valuation.

In recent times, investors have required SPAC to have "skin in the game" by buying extra founder warrants or equity in a private placement.

This financing covers the IPO costs and running costs of the SPAC while finding a target such that 100% of the IPO revenues stay in the trust.

Target Company Quality

The SPAC target applies to an operating company that is either purchased or merged with a SPAC, thus becoming a public corporation.

In certain situations, their equity is sold by the original owners. But more often, to stimulate growth, the injection of capital is used.

Some SPACs concentrate on a particular sector or geographic area, but most have considerable flexibility for target selection sponsors.

Most SPACs have traditionally searched out businesses with positive EBITDA. However, some recent high-profile acquisitions included pre-revenue businesses with enticing investment ideas.

Although the landscape of SPACs in 2020 is very different from what it was decades earlier. Historically, the returns for SPACs with closed business mergers have been much worse than conventional IPOs.

Some investors may believe that SPAC targets have been inappropriately screened or have not been able to gather investment bank backing for an offering.

To counter this assumption, management should do everything possible to ensure perfect financial statements and internal controls.

The most serious risk associated with the SPAC structure is that the company would spend the time and resources needed to produce audited financials and the requisite disclosure documentation only for the deal to fall through.

Reason for failure could be the deal being voted against by a large number of shares. Or even if the deal goes through, cash redemptions may surpass the minimum required by the corporation.

Although the volume of SPAC liquidations has been low in recent times, more deals may fail due to a market downturn. This makes it even more critical to ensure the quality of the target company and prove it to investors.

The Risk for Retail Investors

While knowing and mitigating the potential risks related to sponsors and target companies in a SPAC is critical, it isn't the only thing you need to think about. You also need to consider the potential risks for investors in a SPAC, retail investors to be specific.

Like in the case of conventional IPOs, before the business actually goes public, ordinary or retail investors can't invest in it. However, institutional investors are allowed to make investments in the firm.

The shell company chooses a start-up to merge with following the IPO, and seeks approval from institutional investors. However, there is no involvement of retail investors in the decision.

If the SPAC's selection is accepted, but institutional investors don't like the selection, or they just don't think the share price will grow, they can get all their money reimbursed and no questions will be asked from them.

This promise of "satisfaction guaranteed or reimbursement" does not apply to ordinary or retail investors.

They are allowed to sell their shares, which is a right given to all investors of public stocks.

However, at the same time, share prices may have plummeted, meaning that ordinary or retail investors may lose money on a transaction they didn't have any say in.

There is more. Institutional investors receive warrants as incentives for investing pre-IPO.

Let's suppose they purchased a thousand shares for 12 dollars per share. They may even get warrants to purchase a thousand more at 13 dollars per share.

If the stocks pop to $16, they can enforce their warrants and collect the 60 percent profits not just on their initial investment but also on the additional thousand shares, thus multiplying their profit.

And regular investors don't get to rip open this fun little surprise, as you may have already guessed. There are no warrants for them.

Let's investigate. Both regular and institutional investors originally invest in the shell based on the integrity and expertise of the founding team, firm. It is quite a fragile and dangerous position to take.

Although it still seems that risk at this stage is shared fairly, it is a fallacy. Institutional investors, after all, are not taking much of a chance.

They can opt-out and have all their money reimbursed if they don't like the firm selected to merge with the shell corporation.

They can double down via warrants if they want to proceed with their commitment, and prices pop. The capacity to reduce risk drastically and increase the upside substantially is theirs alone.

While there is an upside to be gained for ordinary investors, it is nowhere as much as for institutional investors.

And although there is risk for institutional investors, it is not quite the same as that for ordinary or retail investors.

The risk-reward ratio between the two segments is clearly not equal. In other words, SPACs are designed for the benefit of a particular group of financial players—the affluent and institutional investors.

However, there is some good news. And as far as initial investors are concerned, it is a fairly massive one. SPACs are a way for companies to achieve liquidity.

This is a huge deal when you sit on shares that have risen significantly, such as by 50, 100, or 200 times. However, because they are illiquid, you can't cash them out.

The last obstacle before getting paid in hard cash is illiquidity. As imperfect and unjust as SPACs may seem, you can't hate them as they are encouraging more and more companies to achieve liquidity.

Having gone through both the advantages and disadvantages of a SPAC, we can say that the pros of going public via a SPAC far outweigh the cons.

As such, you may want to know how you can get started with the SPAC IPO process and what the process typically entails. The first thing that you will need to understand to get started is the SPAC lifecycle, which is discussed next.

Chapter 4: SPAC Life Cycle

SPACs do not have profits, expenses, locations of stores, new customers, or any of the conventional metrics we use to measure the performance of a business.

Instead, understanding the unique progression of SPAC activities and stages is one of the keys to ensuring its success. In other words, it is imperative to understand the SPAC lifecycle to move forward in a favorable way.

Understanding the SPAC lifecycle will help the management teams of the target firm to grasp the complexity and time constraints involved in finalizing a SPAC deal. The following are the stages involved in a SPAC lifecycle.

1. Initiation of SPAC

For the specific purpose of acquiring a business, SPACs are established. A group of individuals with money and understanding of the business will pool their resources & skills and organize themselves into a SPAC.

A SPAC is established by a sponsor consisting of a management team that invests initial capital alongside external investors.

The obligation of the sponsor is to find a private corporation or asset to be bought at a desirable valuation, with the ultimate goal of making this entity a publicly traded company by merging it with the SPAC.

In general, the sponsor will have experience in particular sectors from which the target is chosen and will oversee the selection, procurement process, legal and regulatory assessments, and funding needs.

A SPAC varies from a conventional IPO in that the latter takes a known, privately owned company via an IPO process. This includes a lengthy Securities and Exchange Commission (SEC) application process, including the provision of comprehensive financial disclosures, company history, threats, etc.

A SPAC, on the other hand, does not yet have an identified company to acquire and thus raises money with more restricted disclosure.

In the prospectus, the SPAC will often clarify why they intend to focus their quest for a target on a specific sector or focus area.

The management team often has extensive expertise or contacts in that sector, or at times they just think it's a field where operational changes will provide an advantage.

Either way, in that area of emphasis, the SPAC doesn't have to find a target, but it sometimes works out that way.

2. Formation and the SPAC IPO

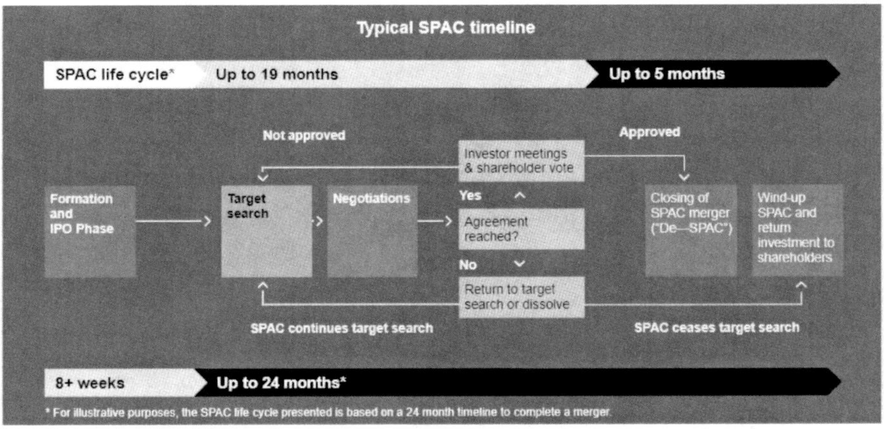

Typical SPAC Timeline. Source: PWC

A financial supporter (or sponsors) organizes a management team in the formation process and finances an equity interest or founders' shares in SPAC.

A SPAC is usually established by a seasoned management team or a nominally invested capital sponsor, often resulting into a stake in the SPAC of 20 percent (typically referred to as founder shares).

Public shareholders hold the remainder 80 per cent stake through "units" provided in an SPAC shares' IPO.

A percentage of common stock and a portion of a warrant (e.g., 1/2 or 1/3 of a warrant) make up each unit.

In general, public shares and founder shares have equal voting rights, except that that latter generally have the exclusive right to appoint through vote directors of SPAC.

In general, this voting right is not available to warrant holders and only entire warrants are exercisable.

Initial business operations are financed by equity investment to initiate an initial public offering (IPO) and identify a planned acquisition.

While the ratio may differ, about 20 percent of the post-offering stock is generally represented by the founders' stock.

The organization will put out an initial public offering (IPO) for investors soon after the SPAC is organized and will explain it in a prospectus.

This public offering enables SPAC to raise funds that will ultimately be used to acquire a target firm.

It is also necessary for a SPAC to become a publicly traded corporation so that when the businesses finally combine, the ultimate "target" can profit from that "public" status.

Units are usually the first security that is provided for selling as part of the SPAC IPO.

Not much later (typically 52 days), the units can be "split up" into their constituent elements to be traded as rights, warrants, and shares.

The SPAC IPO process generally works something like this. The SPAC files a statement of registration with the Securities and Exchange Commission (SEC) after choosing the underwriters in order to start the IPO.

After replying to the feedback of the SEC, the SPAC starts a road show resulting in the underwriting and IPO, the earnings of which are kept in a trust account awaiting an opportunity for investment.

Cash is generated by issuing warrants and common stock. A warrant is a security that gives the bearer of the warrant the right to purchase or sell a security.

Warrants are tradable and have a strike price at which, before expiry, the stock may be bought or sold.

At a price of $10, equity in a SPAC is sold as units consisting of a share plus a proportion of an out-of-the-money warrant.

For instance, a standard arrangement will be for the exercise to be $11.50 with a required conversion price considerably greater than that. In return for acquiring 20% of the units at a concession on the offering price, the sponsor will pump in money in the SPAC and cover costs.

The revenues from the SPAC capital increase are kept in a fiduciary account and can only be issued for one of three reasons:

(1) funding the purchase of the business; (2) to finance redemptions for shareholders; or (3) In the case of SPAC's liquidation, to pay investors if it is unable to conclude a deal within a defined timeframe (typically two years)

A shareholder also has an integrated put option, in addition to holding shares and warrants in a SPAC.

When an acquisition is declared, the investor has the option at the initial investment expense plus any accumulated interest to keep their stakes or to redeem their units.

This offers the investor many options to handle the position before the announcement of the agreement. They can choose to:

- Hold onto the entire unit (warrants and shares)
- When trading at a surplus to net asset value (NAV), sell the whole unit.
- Sell the shares but hold the warrants to benefit from a closed transaction from any possible upside

The sponsor will obtain no reward until a transaction is concluded with SPAC proceeds kept in trust.

The sponsor loses its capital investment if a target is not found and a transaction fails to materialize within the stated timeline, with residual profits credited to outside investors.

In this way, they are given incentives to ensure the completion of a deal and its alignment with external investors.

3. Searching for a Target

The SPAC may begin looking for a target firm that it wants to acquire after the funding is obtained via the IPO.

The SPAC starts its quest in seriousness for an acquisition target at this stage. Often, in just a few months, a target is found. However, there are also situations where it can take years.

Generally, an acquisition is completed within two years from the IPO date. This process works in much the same way as any phase of M&A.

The SPAC specifies and carries out due diligence on possible targets. However, since investors are willing to redeem shares, sponsors need to track cash closely to make sure that adequate capital is available to obtain the aim and handle post-close operations.

At this stage, the funding of private public equity investment (PIPE) is frequently subject to convertible debt.

This is converted into stock at the option of the private investor, thus diluting the equity of established investors.

A definite deal between an acquisition target and the SPAC completes the selection process.

The SPAC team works confidentiality to find a target to ensure that not a lot of data is leaked out during this phase of the SPAC lifecycle.

Shareholders may know that a specific field is the emphasis of the SPAC (e.g. Financial technology, Cannabis, Manufacturing, etc.), but it's just a case of waiting after that.

However, the SPAC does not have an infinite period of time to find a target, as shareholders do not want their money permanently tied up.

The prospectus specifies the exact time duration in which a combination needs to be completed by the SPAC.

The duration allowed to SPAC to complete the search is typically 24 months. However it may be longer or shorter depending on the unique circumstances of the company.

4. Due Date Approaches—Course of Action In The Event of Both Target Found or Not Found

When there is a lot of money the line, things can go in many different directions. A SPAC often finds a target that seems to be a decent match, but then the talks fail and again they start searching for new targets.

On other occasions, the SPAC may not find a suitable target in the first place so things don't even reach the negotiation table.

Irrespective of the target-seeking scenario, when the combination due date approaches, there are three possible avenues for the SPAC and they are explained below.

Option 1: Vote to Extend

If the SPAC has not identified an appropriate target by the deadline of the combination, the SPAC may ask investors for more time to identify a target, and investors can vote yes or no.

In order to persuade investors to consent to the extension, the SPAC can take certain steps, such as offering a financial reward, releasing a "teaser" that provides more detail about a future target, or even just disclosing the actual target.

Option 2: Redemption

The SPAC may "wind down" with a reimbursement activity if they do not find an acceptable target and the shareholders don't agree to an extension.

In this case, the owners are effectively refunded any leftover capital and the SPAC ceases to exist.

Option 3: Business Combination

If an appropriate target has been identified by the SPAC, the firms enter into a business combination deal.

Further filings with the SEC follow by this deal so that all investors understand the combination proposed.

Before it can actually occur, investors must vote on the combination, so they have the final say on the decision.

5. De-SPACing

If the sponsor succeeds in finding and acquiring a target company, in what is referred to as a de-SPAC deal, it would be integrated with the SPAC into a single, publicly traded business combination.

In compliance with SEC legislation, the de-SPACing process mandates the buyer to receive shareholder approval.

The new business would then be subjected to a public company's typical criteria.

Although these laws are more nuanced than can be discussed in depth here, the procedure usually involves the commitment to the purchase of the founders' stock, a redemption deal by which SPAC investors can redeem their stock, and the submission of Form 8-K, which is essentially a transaction registration statement

It includes information to be provided in a Form 10 or General Securities Registration Form, which records stocks for trading on U.S. exchanges.

Since any shareholder may elect not to take part in the SPAC deal, the sponsor doesn't always know for certain what proportion of the trust assets will be required to complete the transaction.

As a result, sponsors are typically expected to enter into forward purchasing deals with some of the early investors to provide additional funding for a deal.

Moreover, via a private investment in a public equity (PIPE) deal, the sponsor can generate additional money.

6. Closing the Deal

It will also take some time (generally months) to finalize the transaction after the agreement is accepted by the shareholders.

The SPAC will usually need to seek investor approval for a combination once it is established, and will draft and submit a proxy statement (Or a joint proxy and registration statement on Form S-4 if, as part of the combination, it plans to register new stocks).

This document will include numerous topics requiring the approval of shareholders, including a review of the proposed combination and governance issues.

A host of financial details from the target business will also be included, such as past financial reports, analysis and debates of management (MD&A) and pro forma financial reports illustrating the impact of the combination.

Once the SPAC acquisition is approved by shareholders and all legal concerns have been addressed, the combination will close and the target corporation will become a public corporation.

A Form 8-K must be submitted with the US Securities and Exchange Commission (SEC) within four business days of closure, with details similar to what would be needed in the Form 10 submission of the target firm (usually referred to as the Super 8-K).

In order to have time to finalize the agreement, the SPAC can also request another vote for extension of finalization.

Because SPAC is already publicly traded, the combination is intended to preserve the public status for the resulting combined entity.

You should pay careful attention to the business merger's terms. This is because "modifications" are often made to percentages, and often additional bonus payments are made, etc. In other words, each agreement is different.

All the rights/warrants/shares are directly transferred to the related rights/warrants/shares/units of the newly established firm when the transaction eventually concludes.

Remember that any "units" are generally split up into the required number of rights, warrants, and shares at this stage.

Usually, if you want to keep your SPAC investment during the merger, you do not have to do anything but wait for your trading platform to stumble over the ticker symbols to adjust.

Depending on the platform and the stock, that generally occurs within a day or two.

You will see a reference to "PIPE" funding. PIPE refers to "Private Investment in Public Equity," which is neither good nor bad inherently.

It basically means that the SPAC will share additional equity with other private investors, which is sometimes nice as it helps bring the transaction to a close.

But it's often bad as it can serve as dilution or undermine the ultimate role of the investors in the new business.

This is the end of SPAC! The shares are transferred to the new, public, combined business on the official merging date and the SPAC disappears into obscurity.

The new firm then begins to behave like a conventional publicly traded business.

7. Managing the Operations of the Public Company

The acquisition is effective at this stage and the corporation must comply with all reporting requirements for public corporations under the Stock Exchange Act of 1934 and subsequent regulations.

For any private corporation, the transformation is a major one, requiring strengthened governance, controls, infrastructure, and operating processes.

However, just because the transaction is completed does not necessarily indicate that the stock of the new firm would skyrocket.

That can certainly occur, but as quickly as it can go up, the stock could also go down.

The market action frequently depends on the enthusiasm created by the new combination and, of course, the newly merged corporation's quality and output.

If the stock of the new business increases for a specific number of days beyond a certain level (the exact price is specified in the prospectus but is typically $18), the firm may leverage the warrants to be redeemed.

That implies that a particular date is presented to warrant holders before which they have to take one of the following actions.

They either have to utilize their warrants (i.e. change them to shares), trade them, or otherwise the warrants become useless.

As discussed above, there are seven different stages in the SPAC lifecycle. However, it may be limited to four in case no suitable target company is found.

As evident from the SPAC lifecycle, SPACs typically takeover privately owned companies via a merger and the former shareholders of the operating target firm become the controlling owners of the corporation that survives or forms out of the combination.

The final outcome is that the former private firm is now a publicly traded company. In this journey from a private firm to a publicly traded company, there are several key players that make the formation of a public entity via merger possible. Perhaps, top of that list is the SPAC underwriter.

In the next chapter, we will be taking a look at the role a SPAC underwriters plays in helping a SPAC become public via an initial public offering (IPO).

.

Chapter 5: SPAC Underwriter

The standard IPO method of submitting a statement of registration with the U.S SPAC Securities and Exchange Commission ('SEC') is what a SPAC would go through, clearing the comments of the SEC and carrying out a roadshow followed by a firm pledge to underwrite.

SPAC will also negotiate committed debt or equity funding, such as a private investment in public equity ('PIPE') pledge, to fund a part of the purchase price for the company combination before the signing of an acquisition deal and then publicly disclose both the acquisition deal and the pledged financing agreement.

Before publicly selling the shares, SPACs pursue institutional investors and underwriters. Underwriters play a significant role in a SPAC's pre-IPO structure. Generally, investment banks assume the role of a SPAC underwriter.

The Role of an SPAC Underwriter

Once the SPAC has concluded its IPO, the underwriter of a SPAC IPO may have different functions concerning the SPAC (e.g., M&A financial advisor, private placement agent, and capital markets advisor).

Each potential new position should be scrutinized for conflicts of interest as an initial problem.

This is particularly important since the underwriter only retains a part of its underwriting concession (generally 35 basis points to be divided between the participants of the syndicate) if the SPAC performs an initial business combination.

Consequently, as the underwriter is engaged in any of the functions mentioned below, the underwriter should guarantee that the SPAC board of directors and, if applicable, investors are notified of this conflict of interest.

As the SPAC looks for and achieves its initial business combination goal, an underwriter of a SPAC IPO may be requested to aid in different activities related to capital markets.

This could include: (i) wall crossing accounts to engage in discussion regarding their views on a possible qualifying deal; (ii) scheduling accounts meetings before and during the period of proxy solicitation; (iii) facilitating the SPAC in preparing presentation materials.

The role that performs the activities listed above is often referred to as a "capital market advisor".

Supporting the SPAC in its investor relations poses possible problems under the rules of proxy solicitation.

It is also critical that the capital market advisor is not deemed to be a proxy applicant because the underwriter, operating as a capital market advisor, has failed to comply with the different rules and regulations related to proxy applicants (such as the rules found in Regulation 14A of the Exchange Act).

As a result, the underwriter working as an adviser on capital markets should consider restricting its operations to ministerial duties.

The underwriter should consider inserting language in these ministerial correspondences revealing that it stands to obtain its deferred compensation if the SPAC completes its original business combination.

The SPAC IPO's underwriter may be required to serve as a PIPE placement agent or to underwrite or organize debt financing.

Serving as a PIPE placement agent may be necessary to complete an original business combination in either case.

The underwriter should pursue its usual procedures for this form of participation, including, if necessary, heading into a separate letter of engagement, including a compensation agreement.

The letter of engagement should contain language revealing that if the SPAC completes its original business combination, the underwriter stands to receive the deferred compensation.

Using such terminology in materials submitted to investors should also be considered by the underwriter.

For a former SPAC IPO underwriter, it is normal to introduce future acquisition prospects to the SPAC.

This is where the previously serving underwriter either introduces the SPAC as the future prospect for acquisition or has the specific business experience to serve as a SPAC financial advisor.

If the former underwriter serves the SPAC in the capacity of an M&A in its original business combination, that underwriter must follow its usual practices for this type of intervention.

This involves entering into a different letter of engagement, including an indemnification deal, if necessary.

The letter of engagement should contain language revealing that if the SPAC completes its original business combination, the former underwriter stands to receive its deferred compensation.

The former underwriter may not want to give their viewpoint on fairness in relation to the original business combination, or the SPAC may not want them to do so.

This is because of the reporting of conflict of interest that would be needed in the viewpoint on fairness.

It is less usual for a former SPAC IPO underwriter to depict the target in an original business combination.

However, the fairness council of the underwriter may be satisfied promoting a target and even providing a fairness assessment (with the required conflict of interest reporting) based on the facts and situations.

This would probably be much more likely if the target is a private firm, and there is no need for publicly disclosing the fairness assessment of the target firm.

If the former underwriter serves the SPAC in its original business combination, then the former underwriter must follow its usual practices for this type of intervention.

This involves entering into a different letter of engagement, including an indemnification deal, if necessary.

How to Evaluate a SPAC Underwriter

The issue with SPACs is that they have two very distinct and substantial life activities: the Business Combination Closure and the IPO, both of which need very different abilities from an investment bank.

And while both the Combination and the IPO necessitate a good relationship between the institutional investors and the concerned bank, a bank needs to have the "appropriate" investor interaction in the Combination.

And by that, I imply key investors in the target's business market or shareholders that like the deal.

In essence, a bank requires being able to market and sell TWO distinct deals with TWO distinct investor classes. However, it is important for me to clarify a few key things here, which are as under.

Selling the IPO

The first thing of note is that you need to sell the offer at the IPO, and when it comes to selling the offer for very big SPACs, that is not a simple job.

Oddly, due to the "perceived value," it is often much tougher when they're small.

Perceive value pricing is a technique in which you set a price where you believe a consumer is psychologically happy.

For example, if it is too inexpensive, the buyer will consider the item as less desirable than a more costly and comparable item and would not want to purchase it.

There are, however, a variety of organizations that have historically invested (and recognize) SPACs, so the method of selling an IPO is arguably a bit simpler than the market combination

However, the combination does not really matter to quite a significant number of institutional SPAC investors and here's where things can get tricky.

They are part of the IPO for trading the warrant (and right if it is included) and will claim the amount of redemption or conversion pro rata through the Share in trust.

They have thus locked in a yield through the share and have the option of selling or using the warrant.

These investors, those that the bank already recognizes can convert or redeem right from the beginning, ought to be "recycled" or replaced by more simple investors or investors who prefer the firm/industry/combination and want to buy the stock.

Marketing the Business Combination

A SPAC does not need to use the IPO underwriter to sell the combination, which further complicates matters.

In fact, an investment bank can potentially do a fair volume of business as a "Capital Markets Advisor" to the Business Combinations.

After introducing a combination to operate in precisely this capacity, several SPACs have called in additional banks.

But we're talking about extra fees now....and a Capital Markets Advisor isn't cheap because it's arguably the most challenging and significant task in the life of a SPAC.

They must market the transaction of a SPAC in such a way that the depletion of cash in trust to converting/redeeming investors is reduced.

They do this by recycling or changing investors who want to exit or persuading current shareholders to stay put. It is important that an "expert" in SPACs is a Capital Markets Advisor.

But going back to how are we assessing a SPAC bank. Are we separating the SPAC life events and individually evaluating the IPO and Business Combination abilities? I think no, that wouldn't be right.

Instead, the ideal underwriter for a SPAC would be someone that can handle both the Business Combination and the IPO equally well.

And in the industry in which SPAC is pursuing, they should also have good experience and expertise.

SECTOR FOCUS

A Business Combination does not necessarily need to be found by a SPAC in its preferred sector focus.

The language in prospectuses clearly indicates that a SPAC can search any industry or geographical area. Despite this, it may have a "preference" for a specific industry, etc.

Plus, there are SPACs with a generic or wide-ranging mandate. They say they have no preference and they're going to look into all.

So let's say you're an Energy SPAC, you can look at any business in any field, but the history of your management team is well suited to oil & gas, and that's your choice.

Therefore, you go out and pursue a brilliant SPAC underwriter who also has energy experience.

You do this because you believe their capital markets will have the "appropriate" investors and ideally, their energy analysis specialist will cover you as a business combo firm.

And then, suppose you find your ideal deal (or you're running out of time) and you have to settle for another sector. In either case, the deal you find is in another sector…say Fintech. Now what?

As you can see, it's very difficult to assess a SPAC underwriter. A SPAC should prepare for the best, but prepare for the unexpected as well.

Underwriting Discount Structure in SPAC IPOs

SPAC IPOs have a unique underwriting discount model. The underwriters usually earn a concession of 5%-7% of the gross IPO revenues in a conventional IPO, which they deduct from the revenues provided at closing.

The standard discount arrangement in a SPAC IPO is for 2% of the gross revenues to be paid at the closing of the IPO, with another 3.5% being credited into the trust account and due to the underwriters at the close of the De-SPAC deal.

The deferred 3.5 percent discount is never provided to the underwriters if no De-SPAC transaction takes place and is used with the remainder of the trust account balance to reimburse the public shares.

A lock-up arrangement for 180 days from the pricing of the IPO is signed by the officers, directors, and sponsors in a conventional IPO.

The standard lock-up for a SPAC IPO lasts for up to one year from the closure of the De-SPAC deal, subject to early removal if the common shares are trading over a fixed price (typically $12.00 per share) for twenty out of thirty trading days beginning 150 days after the De-SPAC deal is completed.

The Need of Director and Officer (D&O) Underwriting

The IPO process generates a lot of cash for a SPAC, but that capital is kept in a trust. There is a much lower percentage of working capital, supported by the sponsors of the SPAC, to be used for all the costs of the SPAC. The D&O insurance cost is one such critical cost.

The cost of D&O insurance for SPACs has risen significantly from the start of 2020 to the start of the fourth quarter, as have the self-insured retention benefits (like a deductible).

The cost of a typical $20 million D&O insurance program was about $350,000 in Jan 2020. The cost of the same program had increased to approximately $1.1 million by the third quarter of 2020.

Why was there a sudden increase in costs?

The number of SPAC IPOs, all of which require D&O protection, is a major factor.

Over 150 of these blank check companies had gone public in 2020 by October 20, 2020, as per SPACInsider, generating upwards of $50 billion in revenues. (Insider, 2020)

For SPAC IPOs, there is limited insurance capital available. So, it's no wonder that costs are rising as demand grows.

Moreover, such a high degree of industry activity carries with it the potential for more lawsuits by shareholders.

D&O insurance carriers are worried because their money would be restricted if shareholders bring litigation alleging wrongful actions by the directors and officers of a SPAC.

Underwriters are also worried that the large amount of SPACs will encourage review of the Securities and Exchange Commission.

No applicant lawsuit against a SPAC IPO has been filed to date. As such, an accomplished insurance broker would be able to negotiate D&O coverage with significantly more favorable rates and SIRs than those of a traditional IPO scheme, even with rising costs.

That said, for SPAC IPOs, the D&O insurance marketplace is actually more restricted than for conventional operating firms.

For certain insurers, the blank-check nature is hard to model in their underwriting. There is confusion about where the trust's resources will be invested, and considering their re-insurance treaties, many carriers are reluctant to issue long-term policies.

Several factors make it difficult for certain carriers who can write D&O insurance for operating company IPOs to quote a SPAC policy. These include:

- On a multi-year basis, usually 24 months, a SPAC D&O policy is written to span the duration of the due diligence phase of the SPAC
- The program should include pre-agreed run-off or "tail" policy expenses and conditions to be effective when the market combination is closed. 'Tail' policies have an extended period of time, usually six years, to report claims for incidents that happened while the initial policy was in place. Preferably, any unearned premium should be repaid on a pro-rata basis if a de SPAC transaction occurs before the end of the IPO agreement.

Of course, the fact that all D&O insurance companies do not offer these vital terms limits the insurance capital available for SPAC IPOs, another reason why premiums continue to increase.

Key Underwriting Factors for SPAC IPOs

The following are some key considerations for underwriters when determining how much to charge for director and officers (D&O) insurance in a SPAC IPO.

1. The Background of the Sponsor

The underwriters would reflect on the makeup of the board of directors and management team of the SPAC when evaluating the S-1.

The background, investing history and credibility of each member of the group in their particular industry and the SPAC field will be evaluated.

Compared to one comprised of less experienced members or those who have not engaged in a SPAC project before, a sponsor team made up of experienced SPAC veterans who have carried out numerous SPAC deals may be seen as a more appealing risk.

Moreover, insurance underwriters are suspicious about any SPAC officers or directors who may be noted for irregular conduct, and their services/interest would be priced accordingly.

2. *Expected Fundraise Amount*

The bigger the fundraiser, the greater the premium for D&O policy and -insured retention. Settlement sums in securities class action suits have traditionally been aligned with the market cap of a firm.

Thus, as an example, SPAC of $100 million would get quotes for D&O insurance with a lower premium and SIRs than a SPAC that is equal to or greater than $500 million.

3. *Target Class of Business for Acquisition and Alignment with Sponsor Experience*

Insurance underwriters would like to see a connection between the skills of the sponsor team and the identified category of potential businesses to acquire.

A board of individuals with a track history of investing in and running similar companies planning to do businesses in the same area would be treated favorably.

However, a team with relevant sector expertise that otherwise wants to invest resources in any other industry would be seen more negatively.

It should also be remembered that regardless of who is on the board, certain sectors are challenging; an example of this would be anything that has to do with cannabis.

4. *Target Business Geography*

D&O insurance carriers favor writing policies in regions and states where they know the laws of the state, corporate security laws and the landscape of the consumer economy.

Different insurers have stringent rules that stop them from covering regions where they do not have this knowledge and insight.

SPACs targeting companies in the United States, for instance, will find things less challenging with insurance underwriters than those trying to target companies in China.

In addition, certain domestic insurers can only write D&O policies for firms based in the United States.

5. *Specificity of the Target Criteria Provided in the S-1*

The underwriters try to predict where the cash injection into the SPAC will ultimately be utilized in a transaction when reviewing the S-1

The more precise the details on the target business class and its location presented in the S-1 registration statement, the more confident the insurance underwriters are likely to be regarding the reliability of the information provided.

Therefore, underwriters would be more secure in their ability to interpret the reach of a SPAC's future acquisitions involving a "SaaS tech firm based in North America" as opposed to if the target description simply read "a tech firm without a worldwide location preference."

Being more precise about the target business class provides insurance underwriters with the ability to supply their rating system with extra credits.

6. *Federal Forum Provisions*

D&O subscribers will request the incorporation of federal forum requirements in the corporate charter records of the SPAC.

An S-1 that specifically contains provisions of the federal forum would be deemed advantageous.

Insurance carriers will need assurance that the rules of the federal forum are shown in the charter documentation of the SPAC if it is not clear from the S-1.

If the provisions were not included in the charter papers, the underwriters would be less equipped to offer risk coverage.

7. Potential Conflicts of Interest

When evaluating the SPAC profile, the insurance carriers would want to ensure that there are no conceivable potential conflicts in the relationships between the sponsors and the SPAC.

If the underwriters consider the "promote" or any other compensation earned by management to fund the SPAC to be too high, they would most likely hesitate to offer terms.

Additionally, the underwriters will evaluate the reporting of related party transactions.

For instance, carriers would like to avoid situations where sponsors buy a business where a director or officer has a previously defined connection to the target and would profit from the deal.

There would be less enthusiasm from the underwriters if there were any other provisions that could trigger doubt, such as an unusual warrant structure.

8. Advisory Team

Just like the history of the sponsor, the better the advisory team of the SPAC, the more confident the underwriters would be in writing the risk.

This group involves the external counsel of the SPAC, auditors, and investment bankers.

A SPAC would want to partner with reputable companies with a lot of experience in the comfort insurance business.

This is because these companies would have spent time and money to carry out their own due diligence.

The SPAC is laying the groundwork for as effective an IPO launch as possible by seeking such assistance.

Some SPACs May As Risky As Traditional IPO Companies

Although some D&O insurance underwriters currently see SPACs as less risky than the conventional IPO firm, a few others do not hold the same viewpoint.

Also, D&O insurance carriers follow the environment closely to write business in the industry.

Nevertheless, amid already high rates, many carriers claim that the price of D&O insurance for SPAC IPOs continue to be underpriced.

These carriers can only start writing policies if they are willing to charge even higher rates and withholdings.

This is something that some SPACs will need to consider in the future if capacity becomes any more limited than it is now.

Despite the risks and complexities associated with some SPACs that may cause underwriters to come up with a higher fee for D &O insurance, SPACs are seen as an attractive investment.

The SPAC investor and everything that goes into the decision of investing in a SPAC IPO are discussed next.

.

Chapter 6: SPAC Investor

A SPAC is typically established by a group of investors with a strong history in a specific industry or business field; these investors are referred to as sponsors.

They generate capital through other investors and use it to acquire an established business, which is privately owned, and then take it publicly in an IPO.

The sponsors normally either do not have a clear objective in mind when they launch the SPAC or are not ready to call it in order to escape the detailed documentation and reporting mandated by the Securities and Exchange Commission (SEC).

Usually, the initial underwriters and institutional investors, and the individual investors who normally come in later, have no way of knowing for sure how the sponsors will allocate the capital.

So, in the hope of nabbing a sound investment, early investors essentially rely on the credibility of the sponsors.

However, the investors need to be ready to wait. It may take up to two years to select and publicly introduce the target company it wants to acquire or theoretically combine with, even after a SPAC goes public (as per SEC rules, the corporate charter defines the exact time period).

The SPAC is liquidated if that does not happen, and funds generated by it are expected to be reimbursed to investors.

All of this confusion is one reason why most SPACs sell at just $10 a share.

Of course, the expectation is that the share prices will skyrocket when and if they acquire a business and take it public. Investors can cash out at this stage or hang on for longer-term profits.

Understanding SPAC from an Investment Perspective

In 2020, special purpose acquisition companies (SPACs) experienced a boom.

A SPAC is a public shell corporation established to complete a business merger with a private operating firm within a defined period of time.

Merging with an already public shell, the private corporation will effectively accomplish an IPO at a lower cost than a conventional IPO with a preserved public shareholder base. It can also provide greater confidence in a deal in difficult times.

SPAC founders have an enticing upside opportunity for a surprisingly low capital investment, frequently owning 20% or more of the residual equity of a SPAC immediately after its IPO in the shape of so-called "founders' shares".

This comes along with a large number of warrants acquired in a private placement.

Following the company combination, owners of SPAC IPO shares also have promising prospects and receive downside protection.

This is because, upon completion of a business combination, the IPO earnings are usually deposited in a trust account, and holders of the IPO shares can redeem the shares at the time of the business merger.

A SPAC must also refund the funds kept in that trust account if it does not conclude a business combination within a defined period of time.

Due to its ever-increasing popularity, many investors want to get into the SPAC market.

However, anyone wanting to enter this market would do well to understand exactly what they are getting into. This will save you (the investor) from unnecessary problems later on.

Buying the IPO Shares

In its IPO, a SPAC usually issues units comprising of one share of stock and a portion of a warrant.

In general, SPAC non-affiliates can sell these units easily on the public market after the IPO.

The warrants and common stock will start selling separately shortly after the IPO and will continue being easily traded by non-affiliates.

Suppose the issuer does not complete a business merger within a certain permitted period of time (generally 18-24 months). In that case, the SPAC will reimburse the money in the trust account for any shares issued in its IPO and the warrants will expire meaninglessly.

Usually, the warrants will not be executed until 1 year after the IPO and thirty days after the business merger.

Although the SPAC shares are 'beneficially held' by investors until they are acquired for the reasons of Section 13(d), the warrants do not lead directly to the beneficial ownership of the underlying stock until the requirements for their exercise (i.e. company merger and registration) have been met.

As a SPAC investor, it is critical for you to understand how to determine your beneficial ownership.

This is important not only for the reasons of Section 13(d) reporting but also for recognizing the potential to cause Section 16 reporting and short-swing benefit disgorgement problems when you transact in the SPAC stocks.

Investments in the Sponsor Vehicle

Many SPAC founders establish sponsor vehicles to preserve their warrants and shares.

Investments in the SPAC sponsor vehicle can provide shareholders with discreet investment interest in the founders' shares of the sponsor of the SPAC and warrants of private placement.

Usually, these founders' holdings and/or private placement warrants are then issued to shareholders in the sponsor vehicle until any applicable lock-ups expire after the business merger.

Usually, the founders' shares are not refundable with the funds in the trust account. Still, they provide an incredibly low cost basis and usually offer most of the benefit allowed to the founders of a SPAC.

Usually, the private placement warrants and founders' shares are also reported for resale after the merger.

For SPACs, registration is especially necessary since Rule 144 is not accessible for the selling of SPAC shares until one year after the business combination of the SPAC.

This implies that registration before that time is the only choice for those seeking to sell a SPAC's limited or regulated securities on the stock market.

Usually, non-controlling shareholders in the sponsor vehicle will not have beneficial ownership of any shares held for reasons of Section 13(d) by the sponsor vehicle until and unless they are allocated.

However, it is critical to consider how the investor will eventually be impacted by this ownership.

FORWARD PURCHASE AGREEMENTS AND THE BUSINESS COMBINATION PIPE

Another manner in which investors are exposed to SPACs is by investing in a funds generation at the time of the merger.

Some investors enter into a forward purchasing arrangement with the SPAC at the point of the IPO undertaking to inject additional capital in the SPAC at the time of the business merger.

At the point the business merger is being discussed, some agree to partake in a PIPE agreement that is carried out simultaneously with the processing of the merger.

In order to get their stocks listed for resale, these investors eventually buy unregistered stock, often with warrants, and obtain registration rights.

Again, this registration is necessary as it is the only way to sell before Rule 144 becomes accessible on the stock market.

Details about the planned business merger (and PIPE) will be provided to these shareholders before they are publicly disclosed and excluded from trading.

Investors with interest in public market trading should assess the impact of being confined before breaching the wall.

While it is definitely an opportune time in the world of SPAC investments, certain criterion needs to be met.

This includes having knowledge of the liquidity profile and what you are purchasing.

Additionally, investors need to know the regulatory repercussions along the way to be able to navigate these investments appropriately.

How SPAC Investment Differs From Investment in a Traditional IPO

SPACs are becoming a popular vehicle for different transactions, including the change from a private company to a publicly listed corporation.

Some market participants argue that, compared to conventional initial public offerings, or IPOs, a private company will become a publicly traded company in a SPAC exchange with greater clarity regarding pricing and influence over the terms of the deal.

Most often when a SPAC acquires or combines with a private corporation, these kinds of transactions happen after the SPAC has concluded its own IPO, often several months or more than a year after that.

A SPAC is a shell corporation when it becomes public. This is different from an operating company that becomes public through a conventional IPO.

This implies that the SPAC does not have an existing operating business and has no assets other than cash and small investments, including IPO revenues.

You depend on the management team that established the SPAC, often alluded to as the sponsor(s), if you invest in a SPAC at the IPO level, as the SPAC seeks to acquire or merge with an existing company.

This merger or acquisition is referred to as the initial business combination.

A SPAC may specify a particular industry or sector in its IPO prospectus that it will pursue as it tries to merge with an operating company, but it is not obliged to look for a target in the sector specified.

Once the SPAC has established an initial business merger opportunity, its leadership enters the discussion with the operating company and performs the business combination if accepted by the SPAC shareholders (if an investor vote is needed).

This deal is typically organized as a reverse merger in which the operating company combines with the SPAC or a division of the SPAC and merges therein.

Although the original business merger can be organized in different ways, after the deal, the merged entity is a publicly traded company. It takes on the business of the target operating company.

Things Investors Must Know Before the Initial Business Combination

There are a variety of things to consider when contemplating an investment in a SPAC.

For example, whether you participate in a SPAC by investing in its IPO or by buying its shares on the open market after an IPO, you must thoroughly read the IPO prospectus of the SPAC.

You must also carefully go through its regular and current reports submitted to the SEC in compliance with its ongoing reporting requirements.

The conditions of your investment are crucial to understand. SPACs can often be similarly organized and may be subjected to certain basic exchange listing criteria.

Despite this, it is crucial to understand the specific characteristics of an individual SPAC, including the sponsor's own equity interests that may have been acquired for limited consideration.

Furthermore, since the SPAC does not have an operational history to analyze, it is necessary to examine the corporate record of the leadership of SPAC and its sponsors.

The SEC's EDGAR database is where you can check the SPAC IPO prospectus and regular and existing reports.

From an investor viewpoint, the following are some of the most important things to know before an initial business combination.

Trust Account

Usually, SPAC IPO revenues minus revenue used for some fees and costs are kept in a trust account.

A third party holds the money before the deal is finalized, equivalent to an escrow agreement when purchasing a property—in the case of a SPAC, the original business combination—or the SPAC is liquidated for not having concluded an initial business combination within a specified time period.

In general, SPACs invest the revenues in reasonably secure, interest-bearing investment vehicles.

However, the precise terms of the offer should be closely checked because there is no law requiring the revenues to be invested only in certain types of vehicles.

SPACs typically use the interest on trust account investments to pay taxes.

A SPAC gives its investors the ability to redeem their holdings connected with a corporate merger rather than simply being a shareholder in the merged entity.

If the SPAC does not complete a business merger, the investors shall be beneficiaries of the trust and shall have the right to their pro rata share of the net balance upon investment in the trust account.

One thing to remember is that you are only eligible for the pro rata share of the trust account if you bought the stock on the open market and not the rate at which you acquired the SPAC shares on the exchange.

For instance, if a SPAC conducted an IPO at $15 per share, but you acquired 100 SPAC shares at $16 per share on the open market, the stocks you buy are connected to a trust account balance of approximately $15 per share.

So your trust account share will be worth around $1500, rather than the $1600 you've paid for your stock.

To be clear about the conditions of the trust account, particularly your redemption privileges and the scenarios in which cash can be freed from the account, you should carefully read the SPAC IPO prospectus.

Trading Price

Generally, SPACs are priced at a modest $10 per unit in the IPO. The SPAC IPO price is not dependent on the value of an established corporation, unlike the conventional IPO of an operating company.

When the warrants, common stock, and units start trading, their market values will fluctuate and there may be no connection between these variations and the SPAC's ultimate financial performance.

Period to Finalize the Original Business Combination

A SPAC would usually allow for identifying and executing an initial business combination deal a two-year duration. Some SPACs, however, have chosen shorter cycles, such as 18 months.

The governing instruments of the SPAC can allow the SPAC to prolong the duration.

If a SPAC wishes to extend the time span, investor approval will be needed.

If a SPAC lists its shares on a market, it is mandated to conclude an original business combination within three years of its IPO.

IPO revenues are kept in a trust account until a SPAC finalizes a business merger or liquidates.

If the SPAC liquidates, the owners will be eligible for their pro rata share of the net sum at the point of liquidation, then on investment in the trust account.

It is crucial to evaluate whether desirable initial business combinations will become elusive as the volume of SPACs wanting to acquire operating businesses increases.

Warrants

A SPAC IPO is often designed to sell a unit of securities to shareholders that comprise of (1) warrants and (2) common stock shares.

A warrant is an agreement that gives the holder the right to buy a specific number of extra common stock shares from the firm at a specific price in the future, often a premium to the existing stock price at the time of issuing the warrant.

For a while after the IPO, the SPAC unit will be traded. The warrants and common stocks of the SPAC may start trading on a market independently with their own unique trading labels sometime after the IPO.

The SPAC will usually file a current Form 8-K filing and release a statement informing investors when separate trading will begin.

Investors buying SPAC stocks on the open exchange after the IPO must know whether they are buying warrants, common stock, or units.

The conditions of warrants can vary considerably across various SPACs, and when investing, it is crucial to understand the conditions.

The conditions of the warrants may include the number of shares the holder is entitled to buy, the rate at which the stocks may be bought, and the period within which the stocks may be bought.

It may also include the conditions under which the warrants may be redeemed by the SPAC and the expiry of the warrants.

Investors should go through the IPO prospectus of the particular SPAC in order to understand more about the specific conditions.

Things Investors Must Know During the Initial Business Combination

The following are some of the key things to know as an SPAC investor at the time of the initial business combination.

Redemption and Vote

Suppose a SPAC has established an initial business merger possibility. In that case, SPAC investors will have the chance to redeem their stock and, in many situations, vote on the initial business merger deal.

After the original business combination, each SPAC investor can either continue being a company shareholder or redeem and collect their pro rata sum of funds kept in the trust account.

As the SPAC transitions from simply a trust account into an operating entity, this is a vital investor factor.

As an investor, you can choose to redeem your stock for a pro rata share of the net sum on investment in the trust account or continue being an investor in the merged company going forward.

You can do the above based on how you see the potential initial business merger and its valuation.

Proxy, Information, or Tender Offer Statement

If SPAC requires shareholder acceptance of the initial business merger, a proxy statement will be given to investors in preparation for the shareholder vote.

In situations where the SPAC does not seek the consent of public shareholders since those investors, such as the sponsor and its associates, have ample votes to support the deal, the SPAC may provide investors with a declaration of facts prior to the conclusion of the initial business combination.

Relevant business details will be included in the proxy or knowledge statement.

This includes relevant details on the company's business, which the SPAC intends to acquire.

These details include the company's financial reports, the interests of the participants in the deal, such as the sponsor of the SPAC, and the conditions of the original business merger transaction, including the merged entity's capital structure.

If the deal is finalized and you decide that you do not wish to remain a shareholder, then you may do the following.

By completing the actions specified in the proxy or information statement, you can redeem your shares of common stock—first for your pro rata share of the net sum and then on investment into the trust account.

If a SPAC is not expected to send a proxy or information statement to investors (for instance, if a SPAC is not needed to acquire the transaction's shareholder approval), you will be provided with a tender offer statement containing information about the target company and your redemption rights.

The SEC's EDGAR database is where you can check the proxy, details or tender offer declaration of a SPAC.

THE SPONSOR'S INTEREST

In general, SPAC sponsors buy shares in SPAC on more advantageous terms than IPO investors or eventual free market investors.

Therefore, investors should be mindful that while IPO investors have given much of the SPAC's money, the sponsors and possibly other initial investors would benefit from the execution of an initial business combination by the SPAC more than shareholders and will have an incentive to conclude a deal on conditions that may be less favorable to you.

In addition, additional funding may be needed by the SPAC to finance the original business combination, and such funding often includes sponsors.

As a consequence, the sponsors' interests could deviate further from your interests.

For instance, additional sponsor support may diminish your interest in the merged entity or it may be given in the form of a loan or protection that has rights different from your investments.

You should examine the "Principal Stockholders" and "Certain Relationships and Related Party Dealings" parts of the IPO prospectus of a SPAC to know more about the objectives of a sponsor in a SPAC.

From the tender offer statement, information statement, or proxy statement, you can know more about an initial business merger and the sponsor's involvement in it.

As seen above, the investor is critical for the longevity of a SPAC. The growing migration to longer-term (retail and institutional) investors indicates that SPAC can be a conventional investment option for key investors.

With greater, more basic investors, more certainty of closure, and far higher quality firms, the overall SPAC sector has matured.

The sponsor may use a private placement in public equity (PIPE) to provide the SPAC with extra cash if the SPAC requires further funding to execute the business combination.

In any case, the SPAC will need to be organized with a defined legal structure before it can start generating funds or go public via an IPO. The SPAC legal structure is discussed next.

Chapter 7: SPAC Legal Structure

All SPACs are not the same. Some SPACs are based on executing an acquisition in a specific area or sector, whereas others do not have such a requirement.

SPACs, however, cannot designate individual private entities as pre-IPO targets.

Post-IPO, SPACs put 100% of their IPO sales in an interest-bearing trust account that is normally only available to conclude an initial business combination or to reimburse investors under specific circumstances.

SPACs sell investor units, each of which is composed of common stock and complete or partial warrants.

They do this to reimburse investors for this illiquidity in order to purchase additional common stock in the future.

The warrants are usually priced "out of the money," i.e., at a higher cost than the unit price provided by the IPO.

The warrants and the common stock trade individually along with the units immediately after the IPO.

Typically, the sponsor gets 20% of the common stock of the SPAC (the "founder's shares") after the IPO of the SPAC for nominal consideration as payment after the IPO of the SPAC.

The shares of the founder are generally subject to a lock-up arrangement before the original business combination is concluded.

In a private placement that occurs in tandem with the IPO ('at risk capital'), the sponsor often buys warrants to finance the costs involved in the SPAC's IPO, such as underwriting fees.

A trust account is where the nominal consideration used to buy the shares of the founder is maintained.

Sponsors are usually not paid the management fees until the conclusion of the initial business combination.

As mentioned before, SPACs must utilize their IPO revenues within a fixed timeline, usually 18-24 months, to acquire private firms or their "targets".

Even though some SPACs might have an opportunity to extend this duration (e.g. by a shareholder vote), SPACs may liquidate trust accounts.

Additionally, they are likely to reimburse investors (plus interest) if, within the stated timeframes, they fail to complete the acquisition of a target.

The shares of the founder are not reimbursed upon liquidation for cash, which allows sponsors to find an appropriate target.

The SPAC needs shareholder approval to conclude the planned initial business combination after a sponsor has identified a target.

The SPAC will also give investors the option of either redeeming their common stock for the initial purchase price plus interest or selling their common stock in a tender offer to the SPAC.

Investors can, irrespective of whether the vote is in favor of or against the combination, redeem their common stock and keep their warrants even in the case where they redeem their common stock.

The sponsor will aim to obtain the requisite approvals for the proposed deal once a combination is announced. The combination with the target business is usually referred to as 'de-SPACing,' as stated previously.

The operating company is the remaining public company after the conclusion of the combination.

Basic SPAC Structure

The basic SPAC structure comprises the target business and its owners, IPO investors, and SPAC founders.

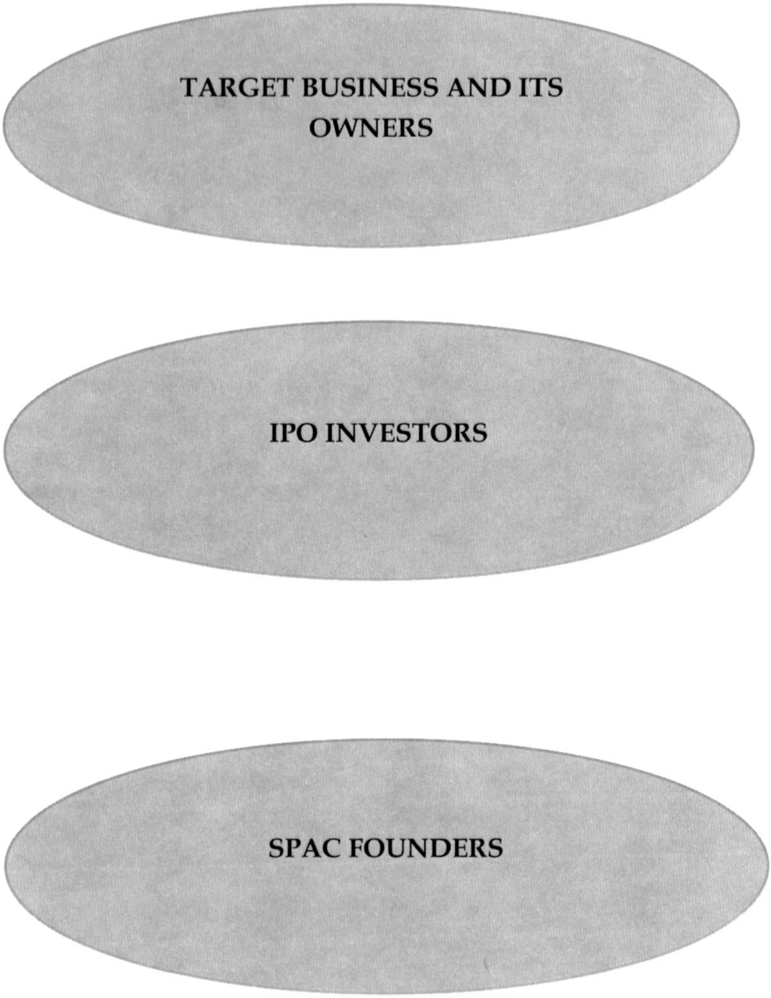

Benefits of the SPAC Structure

The SPAC structure offers benefits for the target business and its owners, IPO investors, and SPAC founders.

The SPAC structure allows the target business and its owners to go public during times when the market is unstable.

Other advantages of the SPAC structure the target business and its owners include:

- Access to public markets
- Existing owners' ability to share meaningfully in future growth through stock rollover that is not available in exit through sale
- Access to public capital to finance growth or operations
- Ability to include financial projections in proxy statement for approval of business combination that is not available in conventional IPO
- Ability to structure transaction, including cash-out to existing owners and earn-outs that are not available in conventional IPO

The benefits of the SPAC structure for IPO investors include the chance to co-invest with successful founders, downside protection until completion of business combination, and investment liquidity.

Finally, the benefits of the SPAC structure for IPO founders include a broader potential investors base and greater ease in capital raising compared to private vehicles.

Additionally, they are provided with a platform to monetize proprietary deal flow and have access to a potentially extremely attractive upside and possible serial SPACs.

SPAC Capital Structure

A SPAC's lifecycle starts with the sponsor. The sponsor usually pays a nominal price for founder stock.

This usually entitles them to 20 percent of post-SPAC IPO shares and purchases additional warrants and shares at fair market value at the time of the SPAC IPO.

Thus, the funds given by the sponsor finance the IPO costs of the SPAC and the operating costs of the post-IPO SPAC in the two years usually allocated for identification of and merger with an appropriate target.

A SPAC IPO includes identifying units rather than of common stock, which distinguishes it from operating company IPOs.

Usually, every unit trades at $10.00 and comprises both a share of a warrant and common stock (or, typically, a fraction thereof).

A warrant gives the right to buy a common share at a specified strike price (generally $11.50) to its owner.

The funds raised are placed into a trust account upon the conclusion of the SPAC IPO. From here, the funds are usually allocated to short-term US government securities.

In the newly listed SPAC, what is the worth of common shares? After the announcement of a target company, owners of common stock in the SPAC have the option of either holding onto or redeeming their shares before the merger is finalized.

Where shares are held, they will be changed to shares of the target firm upon the conclusion of the merger.

The investor gives up his stake of the SPAC when shares are redeemed and instead earns the equivalent proportional interest in the trust account (generally $10.00 plus the interest on the treasury bonds accrued).

In principle, then, common shares in a SPAC can never sell below $10.00 plus interest.

This is because any lower price will present an incentive for arbitration as the shareholder can always reclaim it before the completion of a merger for a pro rata share of the cash in the trust account

Of course, if shares are trading over $10.00 plus interest, it is recommended that an investor does not redeem their shares and sell them on the stock market instead.

Given this choice of redemption, how will the target firm ensure that adequate capital is raised?

The target usually requires a condition precedent to the termination of the merger agreement specifying a minimum cash sum for the SPAC.

Where redemption rates are anticipated to be too high to fulfill the minimum cash requirement, the sponsor of the SPAC may intervene to provide the necessary capital injection or, in a second wave of financing, the SPAC itself could pursue new third party investors.

Such private public equity transactions (PIPEs) occur at the time of the acquisition to ensure that the previous requirements are met.

Alternatively, SPAC can enter into different lock-up agreements with major public shareholders of SPAC to prohibit their stock from being redeemed or sold prior to the date of the merger.

The end outcome is that, with at least the minimum cash provision set out in the merger agreement, the private firm is publicly listed.

SPAC stakeholders (including the sponsor) appear to retain a minority stake in the newly-public firm.

At the same time, high redemption rates frequently leave more than 10 percent of the SPAC sponsor alone.

Securities Law Considerations for SPAC IPOs

The following are some securities laws for SPAC IPOs that must be considered prior to taking a SPAC public via an IPO.

Exemption from "Blank-Check Company" Status under Rule 419

SPACs are intended to avoid being listed under the securities laws as "blank-check companies".

This is because, under Rule 419 of the Securities Act of 1933, as modified (the 'Securities Act'), a blank-check company must, among other things, deposit into an escrow account all revenues and securities provided in its IPO.

In addition, there is a ban on transferring or exchanging securities before a business combination has been completed.

While it has become the market standard for SPACs to deposit funds into an escrow account, it would be an obstacle to limiting trading before a business combination is completed.

The paperwork for most SPACs typically requires up to 24 months for the SPAC to complete this process.

The issuer must offer "penny stock," as specified in Rule 3a51-1 under the Securities Exchange Act of 1934, as modified (the "Exchange Act"), to be considered a blank-check company.

Exchange Act Rule 3a51-1(g) excludes any protection of an issuer that has been in service for less than three years and has a minimum of $5 million in net tangible assets from the scope of penny stock.

To be able to profit from this restriction, the SEC needs the issuer to file Form 8-K with a verified balance sheet as soon as possible after the IPO to show compliance.

SPACs usually use the exclusion of Exchange Act Rule 3a51-1(g) and escape the requirements under Rule 419.

Usually, the IPO registration declaration of a SPAC would state that the SPAC will submit such a Form 8-K immediately after the IPO is consummated.

If an overallotment option is exercised after the submission of this Form 8-K, a separate Form 8-K with a revised audited balance sheet showing the overallotment exercise would need to be submitted by the SPAC.

Usually, the underwriting agreement also includes covenants that enable the SPAC to submit Form 8-K.

SPACs as Shell Companies and Ineligible Issuers

A SPAC is deemed a "shell company" under Securities Act Rule 4055 even though it is excluded from Securities Rule 419. As such, the following applies to it:

- A SPAC is an "unqualified issuer," as specified in Securities Act Rule 405, and therefore may not use prospectuses for free writing (the roadshow presentations are subject to additional limitations without the use of the free writing prospectus guidelines).
- SPAC securities owners may not depend on Securities Act Rule 144 for the resale of such securities until one year after completion of the SPAC's initial business combination and submission of current Form 10 details to the SPAC (the SPAC must also have submitted the periodic reports needed under Section 13 or Section 15(d) of the Exchange Act (besides the Form 8-K) for the preceding twelve months (or for such a shorter time as to enable the SPAC to submit such reports).
- Until three years have passed since its initial business combination, a SPAC will not become a well-known experienced issuer; and
- Many of the correspondence safe harbors under the Securities Act cannot be used by a SPAC.

Investment Company Act

The arrangement of the trust account of a SPAC is structured to prevent the SPAC from being listed under the Investment Company Act of 1940, as modified (the "Investment Company Act"), as an "investment company."

A SPAC is usually expected, following its IP, to allocate the IPO revenues held in trust in either government securities or money market funds that only invest in government securities.

In doing so, under the Investment Company Act, a SPAC can depend on Rule 3a-1. This prohibits firms with no more than 45 percent of the value of their total assets comprising securities and no more than 45 percent of the issuer's net income after tax derived from securities (not including government securities).

There are also no-action letters in which SEC personnel accept that securities can also be exempt from these estimates in some money market funds.

Emerging Growth Company

A SPAC, as described in Section 2(a)(19) of the Securities Act, may be deemed an Emerging Growth Company ('EGC') and, if so, will stay an EGC until earlier than :

i. On the last day of the financial year (a) following the fifth anniversary of the conclusion of the IPO, (b) the cumulative gross annual revenue of the SPAC is minimum $1.07 billion per year (updated every five years for inflation), or (c) where the market value of its common equity owned by non-affiliates as of before 30 June crosses $700 million (or the end of the second financial quarter, if not a business ending December 31 financial year); and
ii. The date on which more than $1 billion of non-convertible debt securities were issued by SPAC over the previous three-year period.

If SPAC (newly deSPAC-ed) continues to be considered as an EGC under these rules after its initial business combination, the firm will continue to benefit from that status.

Marketing and Offering Related Communications Considerations

The following are some key marketing and offering related communications considerations for SPACs.

Roadshows

Any roadshow communication in 'written form' is a free writing prospectus under Securities Act Rule 433.

As mentioned above, SPACs cannot use prospectuses for free writing. "A correspondence that occurs live, in real-time to a live audience at the point of the correspondence and does not occur in recorded form or otherwise as a graphic communication, even though it is conveyed by visual means", does not classify a written communication under Securities Act Rule 455.

A live, real-time roadshow would not be deemed a written correspondence to a live audience, and thus not a prospectus for free writing. This implies the following for a SPAC IPO:

- Conventional roadshow presentations where the SPAC management and the underwriters meet with potential investors in person are permissible; live phone-based conference calls are also allowed.
- A roadshow presentation cannot be documented; live coverage can be used for real-time presentations at the time of transmission;
- Roadshow decks may be given to meeting participants, but they must be gathered at the end of the presentation and participants may not take the slides with them. You may also broadcast slides if they are only available during the presentation; and
- Roadshow decks may not be mailed to accounts or delivered in any way that enables the receiver to hold the deck after the presentation of the roadshow is over.

Safe Harbor Analysis

As a shell corporation and an unqualified issuer, SPACs may not depend on the following safe harbors for correspondence:

- Communications over 30 days before a statement of registration is on file—Rule 163A of the Securities Act
- Research report safe harbors - Securities Act Rules 137, 138 and 139

These limitations expire three years after the initial business combination of the SPAC is concluded.

For communications disclosing an offering, a SPAC may depend on Securities Act Rule 134.

Communications that conform to Rule 134 of the Securities Act are not considered to be a' prospectus,' as specified in Section 2(a)(10) of the Securities Act or a prospectus for free writing.

In addition, SPACs can depend on the rules under the Securities Act on "access equals delivery".

Testing-the-Waters Communications

EGCs and persons allowed to act on their behalf (e.g., underwriters) are eligible to engage in oral or written correspondence with prospective investors under Section 5(d) of the Securities Act that:

a) Under Securities Act Rule 144A, are qualified institutional buyers ('QIBs'); or
b) Institutions which, under Securities Act Rule 501, are authorized investors ('IAIs') that ascertain whether those investors may be interested in offering potential securities.

A SPAC may participate in communications that "test-the-waters".

NASDAQ Considerations

One of the conditions for getting listed on the Nasdaq Capital Exchange ('Nasdaq') is that [the] securities be owned by a minimum of 300 round lot holders (i.e. holders of a minimum of 100 common stock shares).

Additionally, at least 50% of the 300 round lot holders demanded must hold unregulated securities with a value of a minimum of $2,500.

NASDAQ usually needs a letter from the managing underwriter of the IPO to guarantee adherence with this listing provision.

This is done to ensure that the underwriters plan to sell the securities listed such that, after the IPO, unrestricted stocks will be owned by minimum of 300 round lot holders and a minimum of 50 percent of those round lot holders will possess unrestricted stocks with a market value of minimum $2,500.

In addition, within 15 days after closure of a SPAC's IPO, NASDAQ also seeks a list of all round lot holders

The SPAC would have to request non-objecting beneficial holder documentation and a share range review from Broadridge and Mediant following the closure of the IPOO in order to provide proper proof to NASDAQ.

Without more comprehensive details, the stance of NASDAQ regarding accepting a share range review is as follows:

- If 300 round lot holders are seen in the share range review, they will not be happy as they will believe that some of the accounts are held by the same holder.
- If 400 or more round lot holders are shown in the share range review, then that is adequate.
- If more than 300 but less than 400 round lot holders are seen in the share range review, then the call will be left for the reviewer to make.

In the case that NASDAQ is not pleased, it would request that the underwriters include more detail on the investors acquired at the IPO to ensure that a sufficient number of shares were purchased at the IPO by 300 separate accounts.

It is uncertain if NASDAQ will require this if the information is not accessible or there are legal or other limitations on sharing such information.

NASDAQ will count families sharing a household as separate accounts when counting round lot holders.

Therefore, the syndicate must organize book-building activities to prevent repeat investors and avoid the possibility of not meeting the minimum number of 300 round lot holders.

In the event of unintentional duplicate accounts, underwriters are recommended to strive for a 400 holder count.

How SPACs are Different from a Fund

SPACs often mimic investment funds because they invest in a similar fashion, with shareholders authorizing the management team to make investments for them and in asset classes similar to those of a private equity fund.

However, the costs associated with the development of a SPAC and its supporting structure are typically lower than those relating to a fund.

A SPAC does not need the establishment of a fund management firm. This saves the costs and time involved in setting up and ensuring compliance with legislation related to funds and managers.

It should also be mentioned that the investment practices and goals of the SPACs are not designed to accomplish a risk spread for investors.

This is another primary trait that distinguishes SPACs from investment funds.

Stakeholders of a SPAC and Their Incentives

There are three main categories of SPAC stakeholders. These include investors, underwriters, and management.

Each stakeholder has its own motivations to engage in the development of a SPAC, the process of the IPO and the implementation of the acquisition.

The following is a discussion on the key characteristics of each stakeholder and their incentives.

SPAC Management Team

The initial statement of registration and the final prospectus outline the makeup of the management tea and their past experience in the finance sector, previous participation in the mergers and acquisitions, and association with private equity and venture capital funds.

Their credibility, experience and expertise serve as a guarantee that by finding a suitable acquisition target, SPACs would generate value.

There are 6 participants in a typical SPAC management team and they are 51.08 years old on average. (Yochanan & Milos, 2018)

On average, management teams spend around $25,000 to buy the full sum of securities pre-IPO. (Jog & Sun, 2007) (Lakicevic & Vulanovic)

Management teams usually pay a price that varies between $0.017 and $0.047, based on the amount of registered shares while a company is preparing for an IPO.

Before mid-2005, this was the only investment on the management's behalf. At the IPO, management team members offer 80% of their shares to potential buyers.

Practitioners call this discrepancy of 20% “a "finder fee”. The financial literature identifies the finders as the key source of immediate dilution encountered by investors when acquiring SPAC securities.

Mounting pressure from other stakeholders, mainly investors, since mid-2005, and confusion about acquisition acceptance due to the low level of rejection threshold, compelled SPAC management teams to raise their monetary contribution or put more of their' skin in the game.' (Rodrigues & Stegemoller, 2014).

Management members buy warrants before the IPO and, in some situations, even procure additional units in order to gain consent for acquisition in the majority of such transactions.

About 2.76% of the funds deposited in the escrow account for the duration 2003-2009 resulted from these upfront transactions by SPAC management. After 2009, with virtually every SPAC, management buys warrants or units or a mixture of both over $5 million to ensure that the SPAC is not dissolved until the original investors are happy with the proposed acquisition. (Lakicevic & Vulanovic)

This comparatively low level of management's financial investment presents a conflict of interest when it comes to acquisition acceptance.

It is argued that any price over $1 after acquisition would mean a good return to the SPAC management. (Lakicevic & Vulanovic)

Thus, in the majority of acquisitions, the management heavily supports the deal.

The financial literature almost universally supports the view that many value-destroying acquisitions are accepted on average and that rewards weighted in favor of SPAC management are the prime reason for approval. (Jog & Sun, 2007) (Lakicevic & Vulanovic) (Jenkinson & Sousa, 2011) (Howe & O'Brien, 2012) (Kolb & Tykvová, 2016) (Dimitrova, 2017).

In general, it is critical for SPAC management to reassure investors that the rewards are properly aligned.

In their prospectuses, most SPACs highlight that their management team members had prior SPAC experience. This aspect has been viewed as significant proof that, once their initial purchase is viewed as successful, management teams may raise capital for another SPAC.

Underwriters: Characteristics and Incentives

In the introduction and development of SPACs, underwriters play a significant role. Many practitioners accept that the creation of contemporary SPACs can be attributed EarlyBirdCapital.

EarlyBirdCapital started as a small investment bank that renovated old blank check companies, organized them to comply with all the regulations levied by the SEC, voluntarily incorporated additional features to gain investor trust and, eventually, to be a securities market maker.

Compliance with exchange requirements and tighter legislation influence the long-term success of similar types of businesses. (Carpentier, Cumming, & Suret, 2012)

In the past, GKN Securities Corporation employed the bulk of EarlyBirdCapital's management team and participated in the 1997 NASD decision that shut the blank check market until 2003.

It is claimed that the interest of the underwriters is primarily due to their belief that SPACs are incredibly interested products in downturn market times. (Heyman, 2007).

As consultants, the underwriters also strongly endorse SPACs. Underwriters also act as SPAC advisors for 47 percent of deals. In certain situations, for their own account, underwriters buy securities and put them into escrow accounts. The overall fee for underwriters is roughly 7 percent. (Dimitrova, 2017).

This figure is similar to the level that is reported in some places for a traditional IPO. (Chen & Ritter, 2000) (Abrahamson, Jenkinson, & Jones, 2011).

While the underwriters were eligible to collect their total compensation at the point of the IPO in the first two years of the SPAC business, the total compensation is generally subsequently divided into a percentage earned instantly after the IPO and a delayed portion based on the acceptance of acquisitions.

In order to authorize the acquisition, creating this deferred portion of the underwriting fee provides an arrangement of rewards between the incentives and managers and potential investors. This deferred fee is greater than 2 percent of IPO revenues post 2005.

There are four members of a traditional underwriting syndicate. SPACs were solely underwritten by smaller investment banks before 2006.

SPACs are roughly five times smaller in syndicate size than conventional IPOs (Aggarwal, 2000).

After 2006, the largest players joined the market. The literature states that Citibank was the leading supporter of the SPAC market on behalf of institutional investors and EarlyBirdCapital for smaller ones.

The structure of the syndicate of underwriters affects the likelihood of approval of acquisitions. (Cumming, Haß, & Schweizer, 2014)

With reputed lead underwriters, SPACs have a higher probability of acceptance. Likewise, the reduction in the size of the underwriting syndicate raises the likelihood of approval.

Investors and Their Incentives

Most investors in SPACs are institutional as per the financial literature on this subject.

On average, they own 78.2% of SPAC equity, while providers keep up to 97% of capital simultaneously (Lakicevic & Vulanovic).

This difference between the level of contribution and the extent of ownership contributes to a substantial dilution. In cases of future conversions and redemptions, the dilution rises.

The amount of dilution reported in financial literature is about 33 percent. Final prospectuses for SPACs estimate that the dilution hit 90% or over for SPACs after the year 2010 (Yochanan & Milos, 2018).

The creation of the escrow account in which almost all IPO revenues are held is how management and underwriters pay for this dilution.

Early SPAC investors may sell their in-the-money warrants and keep shares until the date of acquisition, gaining some minimum positive returns, provided that investors buy units comprising of shares and warrants.

In the years prior to 2009, investing in SPACs was a key strategy for hedge fund investors. (Mitchell & Pulvino, 2012)

SPACs are organized in such a way that investors have payoffs equal to the risk-free bond payoffs in addition to a call option.

They produced an average of nearly four percent higher than the T-bill prior to the global financial crisis of 2007-2009.

The SPACs' literature indicates that returns to investors are usually either marginally positive or about zero during the time between the IPO and acquisition.

This is because investors will be able to redeem their shares and trade their warrants on the market.

At the same time, evidence suggests that post-acquisition gains are significantly negative and, on average, such investors do not benefit from the acquisition support.

Founder Shares vs. Public Shares

Public shares and founder shares are quite comparable in the sense that they automatically change to public shares on a one-to-one basis during the De-SPAC process.

Public shares, though, are general Class A common stock, whereas Class B or Class F common stock is what the founding shares are classified as.

The founder shares are also provided with provisions for anti-dilution and a redemption exemption.

As stated previously, after a SPAC has an IPO, it has a period of approximately 12-24 months to find a business combination, and till that time, the funds stay in a trust account.

The SPAC moves through what is called a "De-SPAC transaction" until the target company has been announced.

However, some SPACs might require a PIPE in order to conclude the De-SPAC transaction.

Private Investment in Public Equity (PIPE) Holding Company

When a SPAC first goes to IPO, they set out to collect a specified sum of money for a private corporation in exchange for taking them public.

However, suppose the SPAC later agrees to take a business public for a greater sum of money. In that case, they will use a Public Equity Private Investment (PIPE) to cover the extra capital.

A PIPE is a tool for SPACs to collect additional money from private investors to acquire the target business in the case of a SPAC.

Shareholders and SPAC sponsors can negotiate details of the form of shares, volume and price of the offer.

It is normal for PIPE shares to be assigned at a similar price (generally $10) to the SPAC IPO.

Due to less regulatory oversight from the SEC, this fundraising approach is considered to be more effective than secondary offerings.

PIPEs are also considered to dilute existing SPAC owners, which is why SPACs have warrants for compensating initial investors in some instances.

Let's consider a hypothetical transaction with SPAC. Say the capital initially raised by the SPAC is $300 million.

However, the sponsors identified and secured a $1.6 billion pre-money valuation and a $2.3 billion post-money valuation deal with the target firm.

The outcome of this would be the targeting firm raising a total of $700 million.

In order to complete the transaction and launch the De-SPAC process, the SPAC will conduct a PIPE to generate a further $400 million from private investors.

De-SPAC Transaction

The De-SPAC process starts once a target firm is identified for acquisition. The process of De-SPAC is close to that of the merger of a public corporation.

Under the SEC proxy rule, in the case of this deal, the SPAC serves as the purchaser and needs the authorization of its shareholder.

More than 20 percent of voting stock acceptance is necessary for most SPACs.

The process involves having shareholder meetings and discussions, completing proxy statements, obtaining SEC reports, and eventually getting a definitive merger agreement.

This process will take anywhere from 3 to 5 months, making it the longest step in a SPAC's lifetime.

In the next chapter, we will take a more detailed look at De-SPAC Transaction and other steps that make up the SPAC process.

Chapter 8: SPAC Process

While SPACs have existed since the late '80s, both the volume of SPACs pursuing targets and the quality of sponsors have increased significantly in recent times, especially since the outbreak of the coronavirus pandemic.

There are a number of things that have caused this transition. First, SPACs are continuously changing.

Today, it is structured differently from how it was a decade ago, and ten years from now, it won't look the same. SPACs' understanding continues to evolve.

Second, and especially important in this post-COVID era, SPACs offer an opportunity to market in a confidential environment using forward-looking forecasts over a multi-year history.

It helps you convey your promise and value proposition via an investor presentation and conduct principal to principal investor discussions.

In comparison, a conventional IPO uses a controlled document based on historical performance, restricts the discussion with investors, and, due to the public nature of the offering, may be disrupted by an unforeseen global event such as the COVID crisis.

Therefore, in current times, going public via a SPAC may be a better option than taking the traditional route of a conventional initial public offering (IPO). The entire process involved in a typical public offering via a SPAC is detailed next.

The Steps in the SPAC Process

SPACs are created primarily to collect a blind pool of cash via an IPO in order to acquire or combine with private firms.

The process begins with creating the SPAC formed by a group of investors referred to as "sponsors". The following are all the steps involved in the SPAC process.

CREATION OF THE SPAC

A sponsor sets up a holding company and, for nominal consideration, purchases founder warrants and founder shares.

This arrangement is typically subject to a lock-up agreement for one year. The founder builds a team and finances operating costs leading up to the IPO.

A board of directors also supplements the management team with deep industry integration and relationships.

In order to begin the IPO process, including SEC permits, marketing and generating funds from institutional investors, this team works with underwriters and lawyers.

The sponsor should put up "risk capital" to cover the expenses associated with the creation, underwriter, and legal expenses of the SPAC so that 100 percent of the money received from shareholders is in the SPAC.

The SPAC is then listed on a stock exchange, normally at $10 per share (some recent exceptions as the structure develops) and trades as a public corporation.

The funds generated are held in a trust/custodian account, which can only be used when the management team finds a suitable opportunity.

Once public, a "shot clock" of 24 months begins where the SPAC has to integrate with a target corporation. Else, the SPAC disintegrates, and the money is returned to institutional investors, i.e., $10 per share.

A SPAC is usually established by a seasoned management team or a nominally invested capital sponsor, often resulting in a stake in the SPAC of 20 percent (typically referred to as founder shares).

Public shareholders hold the remainder 80% stake through "units" provided in a SPAC shares' IPO.

A percentage of common stock and a portion of a warrant (e.g., 1⁄2 or 1⁄3 of a warrant) make up each unit.

In general, public shares and founder shares have equal voting rights, except that latter generally have the exclusive right to appoint through vote directors of SPAC.

In general, this voting right is not available to warrant holders and only entire warrants are exercisable.

Initial business operations are financed by equity investment to initiate an initial public offering (IPO) and identify a planned acquisition.

While the ratio may differ, about 20 percent of the post-offering stock is generally represented by the founders' stock.

IPO Phase

As a shell corporation, SPAC IPOs do not have to report past financial statements or explain assets; the IPO phase can thus be completed much faster than conventional operating companies.

The organization will put out an initial public offering (IPO) for investors soon after the SPAC is organized and will explain it in a prospectus.

SPACs are officially formed when their underwriters file Form S-1 with the SEC on behalf of the management team, indicating their plan to conduct an IPO at some future date.

This initial statement of registration is a lengthy document outlining the process of transforming the registered shell with a standard $25,000 investment into a new public entity that will aim to identify a suitable acquisition goal within a limited period of time.

Form S-1 showcases the new company's funding requirements, the nature of the issuance of securities, reveals the entire subscription agreement, conflicts of interest between the founders of SPAC and potential investors, explains the proposed business and gives the management team's backstory.

Additionally, Form S-1 notifies the creation of escrow accounts where all capital generated during the IPO will be stored, minus administrative costs, specifies how the revenues from this fund would be utilized if the acquisition occurs and if the SPAC is unable to complete the acquisition and needs to liquidate.

Once Form S-1 is approved by the SEC, a series of preparatory steps for an eventual IPO are carried out by the management team and underwriters. Any relevant adjustment to the initial form is immediately reported with the SEC.

Underwriters file the final prospectus, Form 424-B, just before the IPO date, which lists all adjustments that have occurred since the original registration statement.

SPAC IPO Preparation

Two independent parties and procedures are normally underway in the process of public offering via a SPAC: advisors representing businesses and advisors serving SPACs.

In the former, a target firm may undergo a phase to recruit a consultant. The target firm may also equally consider the conventional IPO process or the SPAC process at this point.

As it applies to SPACs, several tasks would be coordinated concurrently by the advisor.

First, the consultant will take the organization through a process called "IPO Readiness."

Here, the company makes sure that the entity has the right employees, infrastructure, records, and procedures to administratively comply with government regulations.

Additionally, it is ensured that the company can switch operations seamlessly to an environment of quarterly earnings reports where the firm can regularly "beat and raise" its analysts' estimates.

SPAC IPO Roadshows

The consultant will prepare marketing materials comprising of the history of the organization and help develop the financial model and forecasts.

These materials will be used in the roadshow process, both for marketing to a prospective SPAC counterparty and to institutional investors.

Under Rule 433, every "written communication" roadshow is a free writing prospectus. However, SPACs cannot use free writing prospectuses.

SPAC roadshow presentations should therefore be conducted in a way to avoid being a written communication.

"A correspondence that occurs live, in real-time to a live audience at the point of the correspondence and does not occur in recorded form or otherwise as a graphic communication, even though it is conveyed by visual means", does not classify a written communication under Securities Act Rule 455.

To say it another way, a live, real-time roadshow would not be deemed a written correspondence to a live audience, and thus not a prospectus for free writing. This means that:

- Conventional roadshow presentations where the SPAC management and the underwriters meet with potential investors in person are permissible; live phone-based conference calls are also allowed.
- A roadshow presentation cannot be documented; live coverage can be used for real-time presentations at the time of transmission;
- Roadshow decks may be given to meeting participants, but they must be gathered at the end of the presentation and participants may not take the slides with them. You may also broadcast slides if they are only available during the presentation; and
- Roadshow decks may not be mailed to accounts or delivered in any way that enables the receiver to hold the deck after the presentation of the roadshow is over.

IPO Event

Underwriters and management structure the IPO of SPACs with units being the security of preference and taking into account historical trends in the blank check industry.

There is logic behind why risky companies should select units during the initial public offering, agreeing to more dilution at the same time by selling more securities at a future date, at the exercise price of the warrant.

Unit IPOs are well placed to solve problems with knowledge asymmetry and allow companies deemed risky by outsiders to demonstrate their true value. (Chemmanur & Fulghieri, 1997)

There is no question that SPACs, as new entrants in the financial sector and similar to their blank check predecessors, are risky businesses and should respond with a risk-reducing structure.

A unit is, by definition, hybrid security consisting of a number of shares and a series of warrants that can be exercised at some future date.

A standard SPAC will initially issue units comprising one common share and two cash warrants.

Recent SPACs issue units comprising one share of the money warrant and either half or a third of the money warrant.

The adjustment in the amount of warrants in the unit illustrates SPAC's development as an asset class under different market pressures.

An interesting aspect of SPACs is that they sell their securities above $5 and thereby escape the SEC rules governing penny stocks and other blank check offers.

This allows underwriters to sell SPAC units promptly after the IPO and, likewise, to market shares and warrants after the necessary post-IPO forms have been filed.

This feature helps investors to openly take part in the process of price discovery.

The revenues from the IPO are deposited in an escrow account with an existing finance company after administrative and other related expenses are taken/

This is where the revenues are placed in short-term high-grade assets (almost entirely U.S. Treasury bills) and are retained there until either used to fund an investment or returned to shareholders in the event that SPAC liquidates.

SPAC IPOs are typically more expensive than a conventional IPO. This is because you generally need to make payments to investment banks between 1 and 7% of what you generated to conduct an IPO.

The underwriter receives 5.5 percent in a SPAC and other expenses may be involved in the merger. For example, you must pay a bank to get advice on the deal.

So SPAC expenses are about a quarter of the funds collected – three or four times greater than what you would pay in an IPO. Additionally, in most instances, 20 percent of the stock is given 'on the cheap' to the sponsor.

SPAC IPOs have a unique underwriting discount model. The underwriters usually earn a concession of 5%-7% of the gross IPO revenues in a conventional IPO, which they deduct from the revenues provided at closing.

The standard discount arrangement in a SPAC IPO is for 2% of the gross revenues to be paid at the closing of the IPO, with another 3.5% being credited into the trust account and due to the underwriters at the close of the De-SPAC deal.

The deferred 3.5 percent discount is never provided to the underwriters if no De-SPAC transaction takes place and is used with the remainder of the trust account balance to reimburse the public shares.

Splitting of Units

Units are usually the first security that is provided for selling as part of the SPAC IPO.

Not much later (typically 52 days), the units can be "split up" into their constituent elements to be traded as rights, warrants, and shares.

Forty-five days after the IPO, SPAC investors have the option to divide their units and separately trade their warrants and common shares.

Forty-five days after the IPO, SPAC investors have the option to split their units and separately trade their common shares and warrants.

A percentage of common stock and a portion of a warrant (e.g., 1/2 or 1/3 of a warrant) make up each unit.

The selling price of the shares per unit is normally $10.00. After the IPO, the units are divided into common stock shares and warrants that can be sold publicly

The intent behind the warrant is to provide extra compensation to shareholders for making investments in SPAC.

A portion of a warrant is present in the units issued to the public, allowing investors to buy an entire share of the common stock.

One warrant may be excised for a portion of a share (either half, one-third or two-thirds) or a whole share of the stock, depending on the SPAC's size and the bank issuing the IPO.

For instance, the warrant could be exercisable at $16.50 per share if the unit price in the IPO is $15.

The warrants become exercisable either thirty days after the De-SPAC transaction or an entire year following the SPAC IPO.

Sponsor/founder warrants and public warrants (i.e. unit warrants) have exactly the same conditions and cannot be exercised till the business combination agreement with an operating entity has been completed.

Target Search, Selection, and Negotiation

The SPAC has 24 months to identify and combine with an acceptable target, although this can be extended by a general vote of shareholders.

When an acceptable target has been chosen, the SPAC board enters into discussions with a merger agreement objective: primary negotiating objectives include target valuation and minimum capital conditions (Including if, in the case of a high redemption rate, a PIPE will be committed).

The running costs of SPAC during this period are funded by the pre-IPO and IPO contributions of the sponsor.

There are no restrictions on the type of company a SPAC can acquire, though many will highlight a target industry before IPO.

Subsequently, an operating company can merge with, or be acquired by, the publicly traded SPAC and become a listed company in lieu of executing its own IPO.

Typically, the sponsors have 2 years to find and announce a transaction whether acquisition or merger, or else the SPAC will dissolve and shareholders will get their money back. SPACs have two years to complete a transaction or they must return their funds to investors

In a SPAC merger, the evaluation of the target firm is subject to negotiation.

When the sponsors find a company, they then negotiate the terms of the acquisition with the target company, like purchase price or company valuation.

The SPAC target applies to an operating company that is either purchased or merged with a SPAC, thus becoming a public corporation.

Some SPACs concentrate on a particular sector or geographic area, but most have considerable flexibility for target selection sponsors.

Most SPACs have traditionally searched out businesses with positive EBITDA. However, some recent high-profile acquisitions included pre-revenue businesses with enticing investment ideas.

When there is a lot of money the line, things can go in many different directions. A SPAC often finds a target that seems to be a decent match, but then the talks fail and again they start searching for new targets.

On other occasions, the SPAC may not find a suitable target in the first place so things don't even reach the negotiation table.

Irrespective of the target-seeking scenario, when the combination due date approaches, there are three possible avenues for the SPAC.

The first is voting to extend. Here, the SPAC has not identified an appropriate target by the deadline of the combination.

As a result, the SPAC may ask investors for more time to identify a target, and investors can vote yes or no.

The second scenario is redemption. Here, the SPAC may "wind down" with a reimbursement activity if they do not find an acceptable target and the shareholders don't agree to an extension.

In this case, the owners are effectively refunded any leftover capital and the SPAC ceases to exist.

The third and final scenario is the business combination. Here, an appropriate target has been identified by the SPAC, and the firms enter into a business combination deal.

Further filings with the SEC follow by this deal so that all investors understand the combination proposed.

However, before it can actually occur, investors must vote on the combination, so they have the final say on the decision.

Target Announcement

SPAC investors vote on the proposed target after a deal is agreed with the chosen target: a clear majority of shareholders is needed for the target to be accepted.

It will also take some time (generally months) to finalize the transaction after the agreement is accepted by the shareholders.

The SPAC will usually need to seek investor approval for a combination once it is established, and will draft and submit a proxy statement (Or a joint proxy and registration statement on Form S-4 if, as part of the combination, it plans to register new stocks).

This document will include numerous topics requiring the approval of shareholders, including a review of the proposed combination and governance issues.

A host of financial details from the target business will also be included, such as past financial reports, analysis and debates of management (MD&A) and pro forma financial reports illustrating the impact of the combination.

Once the SPAC acquisition is approved by shareholders and all legal concerns have been addressed, the combination will close and the target corporation will become a public corporation.

Once accepted, SPAC owners have the right to redeem their shares in the trust account for a pro rata share of the money.

The sponsor will aim to obtain the requisite approvals for the proposed deal once a combination is announced. The combination with the target business is usually referred to as 'de-SPACing',

De-SPAC

After deciding on the terms of the acquisition or of the merger, the sponsors must propose the acquisition target to shareholders.

If the sponsor succeeds in finding and acquiring a target company, in what is referred to as a de-SPAC deal, it would be integrated with the SPAC into a single, publicly traded business combination.

In compliance with SEC legislation, the de-SPACing process mandates the buyer to receive shareholder approval.

The new business would then be subjected to a public company's typical criteria.

Although these laws are more nuanced than can be discussed in depth here, the procedure usually involves the commitment to the purchase of the founders' stock, a redemption deal by which SPAC investors can redeem their stock, and the submission of Form 8-K, which is essentially a transaction registration statement

It includes information to be provided in a Form 10 or General Securities Registration Form, which records stocks for trading on U.S. exchanges.

Since any shareholder may elect not to take part in the SPAC deal, the sponsor doesn't always know for certain what proportion of the trust assets will be required to complete the transaction.

As a result, sponsors are typically expected to enter into forward purchasing deals with some of the early investors to provide additional funding for a deal.

Moreover, via a private investment in a public equity (PIPE) deal, the sponsor can generate additional money.

The De-SPAC process starts once a target firm is identified for acquisition. The process of De-SPAC is close to that of the merger of a public corporation.

Under the SEC proxy rule, in the case of this deal, the SPAC serves as the purchaser and needs the authorization of its shareholder.

More than 20 percent of voting stock acceptance is necessary for most SPACs.

The process involves having shareholder meetings and discussions, completing proxy statements, obtaining SEC reports, and eventually getting a definitive merger agreement.

This process will take anywhere from 3 to 5 months, making it the longest step in a SPAC's lifetime.

As discussed above, the SPAC moves through what is called a "De-SPAC transaction" until the target company has been announced.

However, some SPACs might require a PIPE in order to conclude the De-SPAC transaction.

PIPE

A PIPE is a tool for SPACs to collect additional money from private investors to acquire the target business in the case of a SPAC.

Shareholders and SPAC sponsors can negotiate details of the form of shares, volume and price of the offer.

It is normal for PIPE shares to be assigned at a similar price (generally $10) to the SPAC IPO.

PIPEs are also considered to dilute existing SPAC owners, which is why

SPACs have warrants for compensating initial investors in some instances.

The target company risks losing a great deal of time, money, and legal fees invested in working on a deal with a SPAC if the SPAC investors do not accept it.

In this case, the associated PIPE funding cannot be raised or, more typically, the SPAC investors may redeem a large portion of the funds in the trust account.

Due to less regulatory oversight from the SEC, this fundraising approach is considered to be more effective than secondary offerings.

PIPEs are also considered to dilute existing SPAC owners, which is why SPACs have warrants for compensating initial investors in some instances.

Let's consider a hypothetical transaction with SPAC. Say the capital initially raised by the SPAC is $300 million.

However, the sponsors identified and secured a $1.6 billion pre-money valuation and a $2.3 billion post-money valuation deal with the target firm.

The outcome of this would be the targeting firm raising a total of $700 million.

In order to complete the transaction and launch the De-SPAC process, the SPAC will conduct a PIPE to generate a further $400 million from private investors.

Super 8-K Filing

A Form 8-K must be submitted with the US Securities and Exchange Commission (SEC) within four business days of closure.

The form must include details similar to what would be needed in the Form 10 submission of the target firm (usually referred to as the Super 8-K).

The SPAC will usually file a current Form 8-K filing and release a statement informing investors when separate trading will begin.

Investors buying SPAC stocks on the open exchange after the IPO must know whether they are buying warrants, common stock, or units.

Usually, the IPO statement of registration a SPAC would state that the SPAC will submit such a Form 8-K immediately after the IPO is consummated.

If an overallotment option is exercised after the submission of this Form 8-K, a separate Form 8-K with a revised audited balance sheet must be submitted.

The balance sheet to be submitted by the SPAC needs to show the overallotment exercise.

Usually, the underwriting agreement also includes covenants that enable

Many of the details in the Super 8-K will already be contained in the proxy statement or tender offer documents of the SPAC for the De-SPAC deal, but extra financial reporting data for the target company might be needed for the Super 8-K.

SPACs are "shell companies" as per the Securities Act of 1933, as revised (the "Securities Act"), as registrants with properties composed entirely of cash and cash equivalents, and the relevant laws and forms.

SEC regulations forbid or restrict the use of a range of waivers, safe harbors and forms allocated to other registrants by shell corporations (SPACs) and previously shell corporations (former SPACs).

In 2005, due to the supposed use of some shell corporations as mediums to perpetrate fraud and abuse the SEC's regulations, the SEC introduced some of these limitations. Based on the individual rule, the restrictions apply to SPACs and previously SPACs for different time frames.

For instance, until at least sixty days after filing a Super 8-K, a previously SPAC is not entitled to file securities offerings under employee benefits on Form S-8.

Moreover, stockholders of previous SPACs are mandated for a duration of 12 months from the date of submission of the Super 8-K to retain their equity before being able to depend on Rule 144 under the Securities Act.

Rule 144 offers a way for individuals who would otherwise be called 'statutory underwriters' (and who are thus mandated to register their equity offer under the Securities Act before their public sale) to trade their equity without registering, normally after a six-month holding period.

Furthermore, SPACs and previously SPACs (i) are not qualified to be well-known experienced issuers until at least three years following the De-SPAC deal, (ii) are restricted in their right to provide reference details on Form S-1 in long-form statements of registration, and (iii) are not entitled to use the “Baby Shelf Rule” for 12 months after the submission of the Super 8-K form.

Warrant Exercise

A conventional SPAC IPO arrangement comprises a common share of Class A stock paired with a warrant. A warrant provides the holder with the right to purchase more stock at a set price later.

Cash is generated by issuing warrants and common stock. A warrant is a security that gives the bearer of the warrant the right to purchase or sell a security.

Warrants are tradable and have a strike price at which, before expiry, the stock may be bought or sold.

At a price of $10, equity in a SPAC is sold as units consisting of a share plus a proportion of an out-of-the-money warrant.

Investors who take part in the SPAC IPO are drawn by the ability to exercise the warrants so that, once the purchase target is determined and the deal concludes, they can get more common stock shares.

The selling price of the shares per unit is normally $10.00. After the IPO, the units are divided into common stock shares and warrants that can be sold publicly

The intent behind the warrant is to provide extra compensation to shareholders for making investments in SPAC.

One warrant may be excised for a portion of a share (either half, one-third or two-thirds) or a whole share of the stock, depending on the SPAC's size and the bank issuing the IPO.

For instance, the warrant could be exercisable at $16.50 per share if the unit price in the IPO is $15.

The warrants become exercisable either thirty days after the De-SPAC transaction or an entire year following the SPAC IPO.

Sponsor/founder warrants and public warrants (i.e., unit warrants) have exactly the same conditions and cannot be exercised till the business combination agreement with an operating entity has been completed.

The public warrants are cash-settled, which ensures that to obtain a full share of stock, the investor would have to pay the full price of the warrant in cash.

On the other hand, Founder warrants could be net settled, which ensures that they are not expected to offer cash to obtain a full share of stock

Instead, stock shares with a fair market value proportional to the difference between the stock exchange price and the strike price of a warrant are issued to them.

The conditions of warrants can vary considerably across various SPACs, and when investing, it is crucial to understand the conditions.

The conditions of the warrants may include the number of shares the holder is entitled to buy, the rate at which the stocks may be bought, and the period within which the stocks may be bought.

It may also include the conditions under which the warrants may be redeemed by the SPAC and the expiry of the warrants.

Warrants are provided to institutional investors to exercise as incentives for investing pre-IPO.

Let's suppose they purchased a thousand shares for 12 dollars per share. They may even get warrants to purchase a thousand more at 13 dollars per share.

If the stocks pop to $16, they can enforce their warrants and collect the 60 percent profits not just on their initial investment but also on the additional thousand shares, multiplying their profit.

The warrants and common stock will start selling separately shortly after the IPO and will continue being easily traded by non-affiliates.

Suppose the issuer does not complete a business merger within a certain permitted period (generally 18-24 months). In that case, the SPAC will reimburse the money in the trust account for any shares issued in its IPO and the warrants will expire meaninglessly.

Usually, the warrants will not be executed until 1 year after the IPO and thirty days after the business merger.

Although the SPAC shares are 'beneficially held' by investors until they are acquired for the reasons of Section 13(d), the warrants do not lead directly to the beneficial ownership of the underlying stock until the requirements for their exercise (i.e. company merger and registration) have been met.

All the rights/warrants/shares are directly transferred to the related rights/warrants/shares/units of the newly established firm when the transaction eventually concludes.

If the stock of the new business increases for a specific number of days beyond a certain level (the exact price is specified in the prospectus but is typically $18), the firm may leverage the warrants to be redeemed.

That implies that a particular date is presented to warrant holders before which they have to take one of the following actions.

They either have to utilize their warrants (i.e. change them to shares), trade them, or otherwise the warrants become useless.

WARRANT EXPIRATION

The expiry date of warrants is five years from the time of the De-SPAC. After this time, the warrants become useless and the initial warranties will no longer liquidate the target firm's stock.

These are all the steps involved in the SPAC process. Now that you have an understanding of how SPACs can go public via an IPO, the next most important thing to know are the costs associated with this process.

The SPAC costs or costs associated with taking a SPAC public via an IPO are discussed next.

.

.

.

Chapter 9: SPAC Costs

SPACs often mimic investment funds because they invest in a similar fashion, with shareholders authorizing the management team to make investments for them and in asset classes similar to those of a private equity fund.

However, the costs associated with developing a SPAC and its supporting structure are typically lower than those relating to a fund.

A SPAC does not need the establishment of a fund management firm. This saves the costs and time involved in setting up and ensuring compliance with legislation related to funds and managers.

Once an acceptable target has been chosen, the SPAC board enters into discussions with a merger agreement objective: primary negotiating objectives include target valuation and minimum capital conditions (including if, in the case of a high redemption rate, a PIPE will be committed).

The running costs of SPAC during this period are funded by the pre-IPO and IPO contributions of the sponsor.

SPACs speed up your journey to the public, alleviate market risk, benefit the firm through better price discovery, and lessen the burden of fees by capping their costs, irrespective of how much capital is generated. However, when it comes to SPAC costs, there are a few key talking points.

Firstly, the costs for going public include far more than service charges and these costs differ for each route taken to get to the public.

You have the apparent cost factors that include money: charges, pricing and the ability to generate funds.

The less apparent costs involving time are: readying the required financials, gearing up your business to go public, and the strenuous roadshow for investors.

Lastly, you have the even less apparent costs of opportunity: maximizing the confidence of investors and attracting the correct investor base.

To add to the above, only when you've gone public previously can you comprehend the latter two categories: time and opportunity. Most businesses do not have this worldview.

For most businesses, a well-executed SPAC combination offers the obvious benefit when you compare the three routes to going public through the context of these expenses.

Most businesses, I say, because SPAC isn't right for all businesses. And I say well-executed since outcomes are scattered, like all financial markets, and not all SPACs are created equal.

The Costs of SPAC vs. the Costs of Traditional IPO and Direct Listing

For most founders and boards, conventional IPOs are generally not the least expensive strategy; this route uses an underwriter – an investment bank – to support the going public process. Plus, they charge an underwriting fee of about 7 percent.

This fee is based on the assumption that they will use their institutional expertise to choose the best price and place to provide the investors with their customer base and make the IPO profitable.

But none of this works till the very last minute because the bank ultimately regulates the mechanism and represents the interests of both the corporation it takes public and the investors it courts to buy in.

The general argument against IPOs is that this strategy frequently works against the business going public, leading to the stock being underpriced and money being left on the table.

The expenses of direct listings are far easier to account for and a fairer offer than a conventional IPO to the business going public.

There is no charge per se since no money is raised. There are, however, large 'advisory fees' payments made to investment banks.

The price is determined essentially by meeting market demand in a direct listing — a very clean, impartial process.

However, as with the conventional IPO, there is no assured access to a quality investor base with a direct listing. You also cannot issue new shares in a direct listing since it is contrary to SEC regulations.

This implies that direct listings are ideal for businesses that are already well-known firms with a solid community of supporters who believe in their potential and have little need for extra capital.

A SPAC is an ideal deal when appropriately executed for the right business, even if it does not seem that way at first glance.

When you compare a standard 20 percent 'promote' of a SPAC with a 7 percent bank charge of a conventional IPO, the fees seem far higher.

However, the fee is a sum of the funds generated by the SPAC that will give rise to a proportion of the company's ownership with which the SPAC combines and then becomes a part of.

The promote shares are locked (for up to one year) and truly make the SPAC sponsor a management partner in the business.

By helping the company reach a better valuation compared to a typical IPO, the SPAC sponsor can easily cover the promotion shares, where the 'price pop' is always the largest expense borne by current investors.

A well-known, expensive part of going public is the post-IPO price pop. It is a thought-provoking time for founders everywhere, who can potentially leave hundreds of millions on the table because of the ambiguous pricing of the conventional system where they have very little flexibility.

The founder negotiates a rate in a SPAC that is based on far more complete data, including forward forecasts and clear, transparent investor negotiations, which is only available via the SPAC path.

And while there's still going to be a little bit of uncertainty, these two variables will easily dramatically reduce the feared price pop.

Of course, the business and SPAC want the share price to sell well and grow during trading—but not at over 40 percent!

The SPAC is in a place to empower the founder in the establishment of prices, as stated above. SPACs will put investors "over the wall" to negotiate future objectives, thereby giving bargaining leverage to both the investor and the target.

They both have a place at the table, which means that their ownership will be covered by a valuable target and a dedicated investor will get a fair rate, which helps to build a quality investor base.

This is where the SPAC becomes a much better option for the business going public, rather than the apparent headline fee.

Another thing worth mentioning is the option for private investment in public equity (PIPE) to generate funds.

The 7 percent charge applies to everything in a bank. Thus, if a $2B firm were to generate $600 million, the bank charge would leap to a staggering $42 million in a conventional IPO (and that is just the bank's cash fee and does not include the price pop).

The fee is usually set at the "promote" with a SPAC, meaning that the business will profit entirely except maybe a very small fee to a bank for helping in the PIPE process i.e. 1 percent fee compared to 7 percent in a traditional IPO.

Financial Costs of Going Public

	Traditional IPO	Direct Listing	SPAC
Fees	7% underwriting fee	No underwriting fee/significant advisory fees	Promote, 25% of shares raised when SPAC forms (such that SPAC sponsor owns 20% of the SPAC shares)
Pricing	Subject to market risk; opaque process run by conflicted investment bankers; IPO "pop" benefits buy-side clients	True market-based pricing	Negotiation between company and SPAC sponsor group, similar to a growth capital round, followed by a market check
Shareholder Composition	Hand-picked by investment bankers, opaque	Market-based real time process	Major shareholders are known to the company before the public listing via the PIPE and existing SPAC investors
Primary Capital Raise	Can issue new shares	Cannot raise capital given	All debt/equity levers available,

	current SEC regulations	including earn-out	

	Traditional IPO			$400M SPAC		
	Offering Fee	Price Pop	% market cap	Offering fee	Price Pop**	%market cap
$2B Valuation & $400m Offering	7% ($28M)	40% ($160M)	9.4%	25% (100M)	10% (40M)	7.0%
$5B Valuation & $1B Offering	7% (70M)	40% ($400M)	9.4%	10% (100M) from SPAC 0.6% ($6M) from PIPE	10% ($100M)	4.12%

One final comment on SPAC fees: In my above review, I aimed to be logical and clarified that SPAC fees are generally lower than IPO fees once you take into account the IPO pop which the faulty IPO system provides to the purchase side.

However, you can also go further and claim that the SPAC charges (i.e. the promotion paid to the sponsor party of SPAC) are not at all compensated by the merger business; they are paid by the shareholders of SPAC themselves.

Much as when a venture capital firm makes investments in a private firm, the costs are charged to the venture fund by the limited partner capital suppliers and not by the business itself. The payments made to the SPAC are paid by its public market investors, not by the merger firm.

Considering this, SPAC fees are much smaller (or absent, you might say) than a conventional IPO.

How SPAC Costs Work

The SPAC generally pays a commission of 5.5 percent of the cash it receives to investment banks, which is ultimately passed on to the corporation it takes public.

For the combination with that business, it would also pay further investment banking fees.

Usually, it offers its sponsor, the popular investor or operator who operates the SPAC and finds a target firm to publicly take 20% of its stock practically free of charge, which is ultimately transferred onto that target firm.

So SPAC payments are around a quarter of the money earned, three or four times as much as you would pay in an IPO.

Like an IPO, at a cost that is likely too low, a SPAC will look to complete the acquisition of its target firm; the SPAC is in business to get a good offer for its investors; thus, it wants to take the firm public at a price that is lower than fair value.

And actually, for businesses that instantly traded up to $20 or $30 a share, some of the high-profile recent SPACs effectively paid $10 a share, the kind of unpleasant IPO pop that venture capitalists tend to whine about.

SPACs also issue warrants to their shareholders, which means the firm needs to give away even more if the stock goes up. So the underpricing impact of IPOs is not prevented by SPACs; they possibly worsen it.

However, you could still push back on the accounting. For starters, SPAC fees may not be quite as high as they seem.

Usually, the way a SPAC operates is that it raises capital from public investors, pays an investment banking fee of 5.5 percent, offers sponsors a promotion of 20 percent, and then seeks a business to merge with.

However, the company will usually get much more than the capital in the SPAC in the combination.

There will normally be a PIPE accompanying the funds in the SPAC; this is a private investment in public equity where the sponsors of the SPAC and their associates will pump in a lot of their own money. If the fees of that are lower, then the overall fees will be reasonable.

Usually, PIPE investments supplement the de-SPAC deal, which effectively adds to the SPAC additional equity leverage. The PIPE capital generation from hedge funds and PE businesses, which tag along for the trip, is organized by SPAC sponsors.

Usually, the proportion of PIPE to SPAC capital is between 2:1 and 3:1. This implies that a $400M SPAC will effectively raise an overall transaction size of $1.2-1.6B.

Fees would be around 20 percent of the size of the initial SPAC (not including the PIPE amount), which goes in the form of equity to the SPAC sponsor, essentially suggesting a mixed fee of 5-6% for the firm as a proportion of the overall capital raised, fairly close to the 5-7% for a conventional IPO.

In comparison to the predominantly cash-driven payments to IPO bankers, SPAC fees are often equity-based to match the SPAC sponsor and the firm.

In order to promote fair prices, SPAC fees may also be activated by results, such that a percentage of the fees will be withheld until the stock price exceeds a pre-determined threshold.

To conduct the de-SPAC method, some SPACs hire external bankers, which may add some overhead cash fees.

In order to make the SPAC offer more appealing to target businesses, sponsors will often waive or adjust some of their economics. Additionally, nothing is fixed about the 20 percent sponsor promotion.

If we can regularly go straight to the retail public and sell these items, what happens if the SPAC decreases its 20 percent charge to 10, for instance? Can a SPAC begin to compete on cost when you actually have this method down?

The traditional response would be no: to go public, you still incur the blank check charge, M&A charges for the deal itself, not forgetting the fee for the promoter.

But in a modern, growing industry that has not entrenched into its commonly accepted margins, you'd be astonished to find where cost savings can be made.

The 20 percent fee traditionally paid by SPAC sponsors for taking firms public may have been motivated in part by the small size and typically iffy existence of SPACS, which implied that it was difficult for a sponsor to find a real home-run company.

As for the SPAC pop—owing to the reality that a SPAC is going to want to invest in a business at less than its fair market value—there is no assurance that that would always be valid.

In fact, it often traditionally wasn't, albeit for bad reasons. They were not really great at sourcing and conducting transactions while SPACs were kind of small and shady; the perception was that their aim was to raise fees for their sponsors rather than making decent deals for their shareholders.

A typical fee-generating tactic among tier 2 or 3 PE funds used to be SPAC sponsorship. While the sponsors of the SPAC generated revenue through guaranteed payments, the investments themselves also lost money, resulting in the deals being adversely selected.

However, that is changing now that large investors are funding big-name SPACs that combine with big-name private businesses.

Nevertheless, I think the dynamic may be that the SPAC is trying to rip off the corporation while the firm is trying to rip off the SPAC, and there's enough history of ripping off SPACs—certainly, it's more prevalent than ripping off IPO investor—to make it seem probable.

You have to persuade hundreds of large investors to overspend if you want to overcharge an IPO, but if you can persuade one SPAC sponsor to pay extra, then you can overcharge the SPAC combination.

An IPO is a Dutch auction essentially; you get bids from hundreds of buyers and then sell the IPO at the price that fits the market, which ensures that the whole offer is priced off the rate acceptable to the lowest buyer.

Any SPAC merger is just a standard auction; you sell your business to someone who pays the highest price.

The community of combination bidders is, obviously, smaller than the world of IPO buyers.

Therefore, the real clearing price for a SPAC might well be lower. However, it could be higher if you can find one supportive outlier.

Additionally, a SPAC is a kind of merger deal, meaning that it can generate value

Rather than trying to make money by purchasing a business cheaply, by buying a business at a reasonable price and then growing its value, a SPAC sponsor will look to make money.

Synergies are present, possibly, in the combination. There are not many because, after all, a SPAC is only a box full of cash; it doesn't really have a business that it takes public to merge with the target firm. However, there may be some.

The sponsor of the SPAC will be a venture capitalist or an accomplished general manager or a skilled player in the capital markets; maybe they will help the business they take public perform better than they can on their own.

The organization and the sponsor, who had once been working against each other on opposing ends of the table, are now part of the same team.

As Chamath did with Virgin Galactic, the sponsor might assume presidency of the newly merged public enterprise.

This is somewhat different from the dynamic with banks: instead of consulting, it's M&A. Your negotiations are more intense, but then you combine once they're over.

The Issue of Underpricing

The SPAC sponsor—generally an investment firm or a popular investor—establishes the firm, takes it public, then purchases a block of shares and warrants. These cover the costs of establishing the SPAC and seeking a combination target.

When a SPAC eventually goes public, it charges $10 per unit, which contains a share, warrant, and often a right to a percentage of a share.

Units are issued by SPACs in their IPOs. On average, 15.13 million units were issued at an average price of $8,544 million during 2003- 2016. (Yochanan & Milos, 2018).

On average, SPAC gross revenues are $135.36 million when the over-allotment exercise is incorporated.

For comparison, one study states that the average size is $116 million for their sample of 2,043 generalized IPOs for the duration 1995 to 2005. (Hanley & Hoberg, 2010)

There is an apparent trend of growth between 2003 and 2008. Likewise, we see a rise in gross revenues from 2012 to 2016. As a result, in the United States, the overall value of the SPAC industry is significantly greater than $33.16 billion. The exact unit prices are $6, $8 or $10.

The escrow account, where the net proceeds of the IPO are held, is a vital piece of the SPAC framework.

On average, 98.01 percent of gross revenues are put into the escrow account where SPACs put more money in the escrow accounts every year after 2008 than the volume of IPO revenues.

Owing to two factors, this was probable. First, underwriters agreed to delay part of their payments before the purchase and those amounts are deposited in the escrow accounts, totaling 2.37 percent of gross revenues.

Secondly, except for the duration 2003-2006, SPAC management acquired either warrants or units before the IPO and transferred these amounts in the escrow accounts.

The level of underpricing is one of the recurrent themes in the IPO research.

The underpricing reported by one study is 3.8 percent, while another finds in their study that the average one-day return for eight-seven SPACs is 1.23 percent, which is comparatively small compared to the average IPO yields for general companies that equals 26 percent on the first day. (Jog & Sun, 2007) (Boyer & Baigent, 2008).

Another study concludes that this less than usual undervaluation is intuitive and compatible with the valuation process. (Rodrigues & Stegemoller, What all-cash companies tell us about IPOs and aquistions, 2014).

As per them, the IPOs of SPACs are much less disruptive, and thus faster, than a conventional IPO. They contend that the investment bank's position as an underwriter and consultant should be less labor intensive as the cash pool is represented by the SPAC.

Moreover, in comparison with traditional firms in the general IPO industry, the creation of the escrow account system makes the valuation relatively stable.

According to one study, there are three critical tools of SPACs as an investment tool. (Boyer & Baigent, 2008).

First of all, SPACs provide the public with easy and relatively affordable access to investments in private equity, which were traditionally only open to institutional investors.

Second, SPACs have a greater degree of accountability than private equity investments, given the obligation to report their transactions and to file daily financial reports with the SEC.

Third, their creative organizational model and the creation of trust accounts, where most of the IPO revenues are kept before the merger is completed, enable them to give prospective investors a minimal downside.

For the period 2003-2006, the study was expanded to 87 SPACs. Their empirical study of SPACs reveals that stocks issued do not show substantial underpricing at the IPO date, contradictory to most of the empirical findings in the literature.

In addition, they report that SPACs provide a less expensive and faster route to private corporations' public financing, particularly in periods of low IPO operation.

Another study uses a group of 161 SPACs and tracks their discrepancies across the listing exchanges for the duration 2003-2008 (Murray, 2014).

The findings indicate that there is no substantial underpricing in SPACs and that underpricing is not a feature of the exchange environment.

In addition, the author discusses the pricing of all three of the SPAC securities and states that the value of the unit does not represent a simple estimate of the stock and warrant values.

Promissory Note

The SPAC shall fund all corporate and offering costs from the revenues of the IPO and the sale of the founding shares and founder warrants.

The (reasonable) attorney fees and charges, printing costs, accounting fees, SEC/FINRA, NASDAQ/NYSE fees, traveling and roadshow expenses, D&O insurance premiums and other additional costs are included in these expenditures.

The SPAC does not have enough funds to pay such fees before the conclusion of the IPO, so the sponsor signs a promissory note with the SPAC to lend money to it before the IPO of the SPAC is completed.

The promissory note covers any corporate or offering costs before the SPAC can pay back the loan from the revenues of the IPO and the selling of the founder's warrants at the end of the IPO.

Managerial Remuneration

Usually, the Founding Shareholders and other SPAC directors and officers do not earn salaries or management fees or finders' fees before or in conjunction with the initial business merger execution.

Additionally, the costs incurred are not reimbursed to them. Monthly room and secretarial and other operating expenditures shall only be paid from the money not kept in the trust account.

However, after paying nominal consideration for up to 20 percent of the SPAC stock, the SPAC management team wishes for deferred but significant capital growth upon successful completion of the initial business merger.

Deferred Underwriting Commissions

Upon conclusion of an initial business merger, SPAC underwriters usually receive a portion of the overall underwriting commissions at IPO and a portion in the shape of deferred underwriting commissions.

When a SPAC is pursuing its initial business merger, these funds remain in the trust account and if none is consumed by the liquidation date of a firm, they will be returned to investors with the remainder of the trust account.

SPACs often skip deferred subscription commissions in lieu of committing with their lead underwriter to a Business Merger Marketing Deal.

Usually, a Business Merger Marketing Arrangement allocates a fixed portion of the revenues to be charged to the underwriter upon completion of the original business merger.

Typically, at the discretion of the SPAC, a part of this sum may be redirected to other financial advisors.

Management of SPAC's Costs

In addition to the offering revenues usually retained in the trust account (approximately 90% of the overall revenues of the SPAC IPO), the remaining revenues of the IPO normally remain at the disposal of the SPAC.

The above is in relation to a SPAC's hunt for prospective target operating firms and in order to meet the general operating costs of the firm prior to the completion of the business merger.

Usually, the statement of registration filed with an appropriate securities exchange for SPAC's IPO would provide specific details on the planned usage of the net bid revenues not kept in the trust account.

The only exception to the above is any money payable in connection with the offering of relevant expenses.

SPACs will usually reserve a percentage of their net bid revenues not kept in trust accounts for things such as accounting, legal, and insurance costs of directors and officers related to current SEC reporting obligations.

However, a substantial percentage of the revenues not held in the trust account will usually be held for due diligence inquiries of prospective target undertakings, together with legal and accounting costs associated to the negotiation, organizing, and acceptance of a business combination by shareholders.

Furthermore, SPACs will generally assign a major portion of their net offering revenue not retained as working capital in the trust account.

Such working capital may typically be used for a number of things. This includes the repayment on behalf of the SPAC officers and directors of out-of-pocket expenditures.

It also includes costs related to the retention of independent valuation businesses and third-party advisors in connection with the assessment of potential target operating companies.

Finally, costs related to the finalization of a business merger, such as the creation of a down payment or an exclusivity payment or similar fees and costs are also included.

These are some of the major expenses to keep in mind to efficiently manage the costs related to a SPAC.

The cost related to SPAC needs to be managed primarily by the sponsor. The role of the sponsor in a SPAC, including the management of SPAC costs, is discussed next.

Chapter 10: SPAC Sponsor

A SPAC raises capital through an Initial Public Offering (IPO) for the purpose of acquiring an existing operating company.

The sponsor, typically a person or team with significant business experience, decides to launch a SPAC.

They create a holding company.

The sponsor also receives 20% of the shares of the SPAC as a fee, called a "promote" or "founders shares."

A SPAC raises capital through an Initial Public Offering (IPO) for the purpose of acquiring an existing operating company.

Then the sponsor completes the normal filings associated with going public through an IPO.

The sponsor then goes on a roadshow, similar to traditional IPOs, to try to find interested investors.

Once the sponsor has attracted enough interest, they sell securities in the company.

The money raised from the IPO is put into a blind trust and is untouchable until the shareholders approve the acquisition transaction.

The SPAC goes public and trades on an exchange like any other publicly traded company.

This is where the general public gets involved. They can purchase securities on the open market, but the future acquisition is still unknown to them.

Instead, these investors are buying on the vision and the strength of the sponsor or the promise of a strong future acquisition.

Once the SPAC is public, the sponsors can begin the hunt for a target company to acquire.

The Role of the Sponsor in Target Search and Approval

Once the sponsors find a suitable company, they negotiate the terms of the acquisition with the target company, like purchase price or company valuation.

Following a deal, the "de-SPAC" process begins. After deciding on the terms of the acquisition or of the merger, the sponsors must propose the acquisition target to shareholders.

The shareholders have the opportunity to vote on the contemplated transaction, whether acquisition or merger, which gives them some recourse if a sponsor chooses a company they do not like.

Typically, the sponsors have 2 years to find and announce a transaction, whether acquisition or merger, or else the SPAC will dissolve and shareholders will get their money back. SPACs have two years to complete a transaction or they must return their funds to investors.

The Role of the Sponsor in IPO Issuance

When launching the IPO, the SPAC management team hires an investment firm to administer the IPO.

The investment bank and the corporation's management team decide on a fee to be paid for the service, generally around 10% of the IPO revenue.

Securities issued during an IPO are provided at a price per unit, representing one or more common stock shares.

As the SPAC does not have any performance records or revenue data, the SPAC prospectus emphasizes primarily on the sponsors rather than on business history and revenues.

All funds from the IPO are kept in a trust account till a private firm is established as an acquisition target.

The Incentive Structure for Sponsors

SPACs offer the sponsors (underwriters) a stronger incentive structure for the target business to collect capital on favorable terms.

Investment banks that underwrite the conventional IPO do not have the same motivations as the business. Banks want to retain their sales relationships and sell shares in firms that are likely to make the most money for their clients.

However, as the sponsors are basically the underwriters of a SPAC, they ultimately have the same long-term benefits as the corporation. It can be viewed as an M&A approach rather than a transaction.

While discussions can be complicated, they're all on the same page until the merger is accomplished.

In addition, when they are positive about a target firm, sponsors of the SPAC place their credibility on the line. This generally results in the firm's fair and favorable valuation.

The underwriting discount payment is usually made as equity options in the business to the SPAC sponsors.

The delayed discount commission helps the target organization and positively influences sponsors to identify a target acquisition to earn their 3.5 percent commission as equity.

To say it another way, instead of paying the SPAC sponsors in the form of equity, the payment that a corporation would make to an investment bank to underwrite an IPO is instead made to the SPAC sponsors.

Although the cost of going public could be more or less the same, in comparison to a conventional IPO, benefits for underwriters and the business are more integrated in the SPAC process.

The Issues Concerning SPAC Sponsors

There are a few common issue concerning SPAC sponsors that need to be considered before deciding to take a SPAC public via an IPO.

First, if the sponsor is not able to draw new investors to cover the funding, the redemptions will reduce the capital available for the deal and render the transaction infeasible if a reasonable amount of money cannot be substituted

Another key concern around SPAC sponsors is the need to find a sponsor with abilities and characteristics that are complementary to the company's needs.

In particular, the acquired business should be assisted by people with comprehensive capital markets, management and board expertise as it tries to adapt to the public markets.

An experienced team of sponsors will also provide management with strategic and organizational support, helping to plug gaps and expand talent across the company.

Another matter that is worth pondering upon is the extent to which sponsors exert power. SPACs pursuing 100% equity in the target business cannot be suitable long-term partners.

The Importance of Considering Sponsor Quality

Initial investors are betting on the sponsor rather than the company. This gives sponsors a lot of power and adds a new layer of risk for sponsors.

All other investors will face immediate dilution after the business merger concludes because of the standard 20 percent of founding shares granted to SPAC sponsors.

However, while the sponsors receive 20 percent ownership in the SPAC, this share cannot be used to redeem cash held in trust.

This implies that if the sponsor fails to close a deal, their equity stake will become pointless.

Therefore, management must assess the potential effect of sponsor warrants, investor warrants, and any private placement while considering the cost of capital compared to other funding sources in order to derive the completely diluted effects of the merger on their valuation.

In recent times, investors have required SPAC to have "skin in the game" by buying extra founder warrants or equity in a private placement.

This financing covers the IPO costs and running costs of the SPAC while finding a target such that 100% of the IPO revenues stay in the trust.

The Obligation of a Sponsor

A SPAC is established by a sponsor consisting of a management team that invests initial capital alongside external investors.

The obligation of the sponsor is to find a private corporation or asset to be bought at a desirable valuation, with the ultimate goal of making this entity a publicly traded company by merging it with the SPAC.

In general, the sponsor will have experience in particular sectors from which the target is chosen and will oversee the selection, procurement process, legal and regulatory assessments, and funding needs.

Obligation in Formation and SPAC IPO

A financial supporter (or sponsors) organizes a management team in the formation process and finances an equity interest or founders' shares in SPAC.

A SPAC is usually established by a seasoned management team or a nominally invested capital sponsor, often resulting into a stake in the SPAC of 20 percent (typically referred to as founder shares).

In return for acquiring 20% of the units at a concession on the offering price, the sponsor will pump in money in the SPAC and cover costs.

The sponsor will obtain no reward until a transaction is concluded with SPAC proceeds kept in trust.

The sponsor loses its capital investment if a target is not found and a transaction fails to materialize within the stated timeline, with residual profits credited to outside investors.

Obligation in Target Search and Selection

The SPAC specifies and carries out due diligence on possible targets. However, since investors are willing to redeem shares, sponsors need to track cash closely to make sure that adequate capital is available to obtain the aim and handle post-close operations.

When the sponsors find a company, they then negotiate the terms of the acquisition with the target company, like purchase price or company valuation.

Some SPACs concentrate on a particular sector or geographic area, but most have considerable flexibility for target selection sponsors.

When an acceptable target has been chosen, the SPAC board enters into discussions with a merger agreement objective: primary negotiating objectives include target valuation and minimum capital conditions (Including if, in the case of a high redemption rate, a PIPE will be committed).

The running costs of SPAC during this period are funded by the pre-IPO and IPO contributions of the sponsor.

De-SPACing Obligation

If the sponsor succeeds in finding and acquiring a target company, it would be integrated with the SPAC into a single publicly traded business combination in what is referred to as a de-SPAC deal.

In compliance with SEC legislation, the de-SPACing process mandates the buyer to receive shareholder approval.

The new business would then be subjected to a public company's typical criteria.

Also, since any shareholder may elect not to take part in the SPAC deal, the sponsor doesn't always know for certain what proportion of the trust assets will be required to complete the transaction.

As a result, sponsors are typically expected to enter into forward purchasing deals with some of the early investors to provide additional funding for a deal. They are also often expected to generate additional money via a private investment in a public equity (PIPE) deal.

Closing Obligation

The sponsor will generally need to get investor approval for a combination once it is established, and draft and submit a proxy statement (Or a joint proxy and registration statement on Form S-4 if, as part of the combination, it plans to register new stocks).

Additionally, they need to submit a Form 8-K with the US Securities and Exchange Commission (SEC) within four business days of closure, with details similar to what would be needed in the Form 10 submission of the target firm (usually referred to as the Super 8-K).

The Importance of Sponsor in Determining Director and Officers (D&O) Insurance in SPAC IPO

The makeup of the sponsor comprising of the board of directors and management team of the SPAC is considered when evaluating the S-1.

The background, investing history and credibility of each member of the group in their particular industry and the SPAC field will be evaluated.

Compared to one comprised of less experienced members or those who have not engaged in a SPAC project before, a sponsor team made up of experienced

SPAC veterans who have carried out numerous SPAC deals may be seen as a more appealing risk.

Additionally, insurance underwriters like to see a connection between the skills of the sponsor team and the identified category of potential businesses to acquire.

A board of individuals with a track history of investing in and running similar companies planning to do businesses in the same area would be treated favorably.

On the other hand, a team with relevant sector expertise that, for any reason, wants to invest resources in any other industry would be seen more negatively.

In addition to the above, when evaluating the SPAC profile, the insurance carriers would want to ensure that there are no conceivable potential conflicts in the relationships between the sponsors and the SPAC.

If they consider the "promote" or any other compensation earned by management to fund the SPAC to be too high, they would most likely hesitate to offer terms.

Additionally, they will evaluate the reporting of related party transactions.

For instance, carriers would like to avoid situations where sponsors buy a business where a director or officer has a previously defined connection to the target and would profit from the deal.

There would be less enthusiasm from the insurance underwriters if there were any other provisions that could trigger doubt, such as an unusual warrant structure.

Importance of Sponsors from an Investment Perspective

Usually, the initial underwriters and institutional investors, and the individual investors who normally come in later, have no way of knowing for sure how the sponsors will allocate the capital.

So, in the hope of nabbing a sound investment, early investors essentially rely on the credibility of the sponsors.

Moreover, SPAC founders have an enticing upside opportunity for surprisingly low capital investment, frequently owning 20% or more of the residual equity of a SPAC immediately after its IPO in the shape of so-called "founders' shares".

Many SPAC founders establish sponsor vehicles to preserve their warrants and shares.

Investments in the SPAC sponsor vehicle can provide shareholders with discreet investment interest in the founders' shares of the sponsor of the SPAC and warrants of private placement.

Usually, these founders' holdings and/or private placement warrants are then issued to shareholders in the sponsor vehicle until any applicable lock-ups expire after the business merger.

In addition to the above, you depend on the management team that established the SPAC, often alluded to as the sponsor(s), if you invest in a SPAC at the IPO level, as the SPAC seeks to acquire or merge with an existing company.

Also, it is crucial to understand the specific characteristics of an individual SPAC, including the sponsor's own equity interests that may have been acquired for limited consideration.

In general, SPAC sponsors buy shares in SPAC on more advantageous terms than IPO investors or eventual free market investors.

Therefore, investors should be mindful that while IPO investors have given much of the SPAC's money, the sponsors and possibly other initial investors would benefit from the execution of an initial business combination by the SPAC more than shareholders and will have an incentive to conclude a deal on conditions that may be less favorable to you.

In addition, additional funding may be needed by the SPAC to finance the original business combination, and such funding often includes sponsors.

As a consequence, the sponsors' interests could deviate further from your interests.

For instance, additional sponsor support may diminish your interest in the merged entity or it may be given in the form of a loan or protection that has rights different from your investments.

You should examine the "Principal Stockholders" and "Certain Relationships and Related Party Dealings" parts of the IPO prospectus of a SPAC to know more about the objectives of a sponsor in a SPAC.

From the tender offer statement, information statement, or proxy statement, you can know more about an initial business merger and the sponsor's involvement in it.

Furthermore, since the SPAC does not have an operational history to analyze, it is necessary to examine the corporate record of the leadership of SPAC and its sponsors.

If SPAC requires shareholder acceptance of the initial business merger, a proxy statement will be given to investors in preparation for the shareholder vote.

In situations where the SPAC does not seek the consent of public shareholders since those investors, such as the sponsor and its associates, have ample votes to support the deal, the SPAC may provide investors with a declaration of facts prior to the conclusion of the initial business combination.

Sponsor Shares

Typically, the sponsor gets 20% of the common stock of the SPAC (the "founder's shares") after the IPO of the SPAC for nominal consideration as payment after the IPO of the SPAC.

The shares of the founder are generally subject to a lock-up arrangement before the original business combination is concluded.

In a private placement that occurs in tandem with the IPO ('at risk capital'), the sponsor often buys warrants to finance the costs involved in the SPAC's IPO, such as underwriting fees.

A trust account is where the nominal consideration used to buy the shares of the founder is maintained.

Sponsors are usually not paid the management fees until the conclusion of the initial business combination.

The shares of the founder are not reimbursed upon liquidation for cash, which allows sponsors to find an appropriate target.

Role of Sponsor in SPAC Capital Structure

A SPAC's lifecycle starts with the sponsor. The sponsor usually pays a nominal price for founder stock.

The sponsor generally puts up "risk capital" to cover the expenses associated with the creation, underwriter, and legal expenses of the SPAC so that 100 percent of the money received from shareholders is in the SPAC.

This usually entitles them to 20 percent of post-SPAC IPO shares and purchases additional warrants and shares at fair market value at the time of the SPAC IPO.

Thus, the funds given by the sponsor finance the IPO costs of the SPAC and the operating costs of the post-IPO SPAC in the two years are usually allocated for identification of and merger with an appropriate target.

The investor gives up his stake of the SPAC when shares are redeemed and instead earns the equivalent proportional interest in the trust account (generally $10.00 plus the interest on the treasury bonds accrued).

Where redemption rates are anticipated to be too high to fulfill the minimum cash requirement, the sponsor of the SPAC may intervene to provide the necessary capital injection.

Alternatively, in a second wave of financing, the SPAC itself could pursue new third party investors.

Such private public equity transactions (PIPEs) occur at the time of the acquisition to ensure that the previous requirements are met.

As mentioned previously, PIPE is a tool for SPACs to collect additional money from private investors to acquire the target business in the case of a SPAC.

Shareholders and SPAC sponsors can negotiate details of the form of shares, volume and price of the offer.

SPAC stakeholders (including the sponsor) appear to retain a minority stake in the newly-public firm.

At the same time, high redemption rates frequently leave more than 10 percent of the SPAC sponsor alone.

With the roles, obligation, incentives, and shares of SPAC sponsor understood, it is time to take a look at an SPAC from the perspective of of the target.

Chapter 11: SPAC Target

Once the SPAC is public, the sponsors can begin the hunt for a target company to acquire.

There are no restrictions on the type of company a SPAC can acquire, though many will highlight a target industry before IPO.

Subsequently, an operating company can merge with, or be acquired by, the publicly traded SPAC and become a listed company in lieu of executing its own IPO

After deciding on the terms of the acquisition or of the merger, the sponsors must propose the acquisition target to shareholders.

How the Acquisition of Target Company Works

The management team has 18–24 months to select a target and conclude the acquisition after SPAC has generated the capital needed via an IPO.

Depending on the firm and business, the duration can vary. However, the target firm's fair market value must be 80 percent or more of the trust assets of the SPAC.

When the acquisition is complete, the founders will take advantage of their shareholding in the new company, typically 20% of the common stock, while the shareholders will receive equity interest on the basis of their capital investment.

In the case that the agreed period expires before the completion of the acquisition, the SPAC is terminated and the income from the IPO held in the trust account is returned to the shareholders.

The management team is not supposed to earn salaries while running the SPAC until the contract is concluded.

The SPAC may begin looking for a target firm that it wants to acquire after the funding is obtained via the IPO.

The SPAC starts its quest in seriousness for an acquisition target at this stage. Often, in just a few months, a target is found. However, there are also situations where it can take years.

Generally, an acquisition is completed within two years from the IPO date. This process works in much the same way as any phase of M&A.

The SPAC specifies and carries out due diligence on possible targets. However, since investors are willing to redeem shares, sponsors need to track cash closely to make sure that adequate capital is available to obtain the aim and handle post-close operations.

At this stage, the funding of private public equity investment (PIPE) is frequently subject to convertible debt.

This is converted into stock at the option of the private investor, thus diluting the equity of established investors.

A definite deal between an acquisition target and the SPAC completes the selection process.

The SPAC team works confidentiality to find a target to ensure that not a lot of data is leaked out during this phase of the SPAC lifecycle.

Shareholders may know that a specific field is the emphasis of the SPAC (e.g. Financial technology, Cannabis, Manufacturing, etc.), but it's just a case of waiting after that.

However, the SPAC does not have an infinite period of time to find a target, as shareholders do not want their money permanently tied up.

The prospectus specifies the exact time duration in which a combination needs to be completed by the SPAC.

The duration allowed to SPAC to complete the search is typically 24 months. However it may be longer or shorter depending on the unique circumstances of the company.

Two Scenarios at IPO

When there is a lot of money the line, things can go in many different directions. A SPAC often finds a target that seems to be a decent match, but then the talks fail and again they start searching for new targets.

On other occasions, the SPAC may not find a suitable target in the first place so things don't even reach the negotiation table.

Target Found

If an appropriate target has been identified by the SPAC, the firms enter into a business combination deal.

Further filings with the SEC follow by this deal so that all investors understand the combination proposed.

Before it can actually occur, investors must vote on the combination, so they have the final say on the decision.

If the sponsor succeeds in finding and acquiring a target company, it would be integrated with the SPAC into a single, publicly traded business combination.

However, in compliance with SEC legislation, the de-SPACing process mandates the buyer to receive shareholder approval.

The new business would then be subjected to a public company's typical criteria.

Once the approval of shareholders is received, the transaction would be finalized within a few months.

TARGET NOT FOUND

If the SPAC has not identified an appropriate target by the deadline of the combination, the SPAC may ask investors for more time to identify a target, and investors can vote yes or no.

In order to persuade investors to consent to the extension, the SPAC can take certain steps, such as offering a financial reward, releasing a "teaser" that provides more detail about a future target, or even just disclosing the actual target.

Alternatively, the SPAC may choose to "wind down" with a reimbursement activity if they do not find an acceptable target and the shareholders don’t agree to an extension.

In this case, the owners are effectively refunded any leftover capital and the SPAC ceases to exist.

Target Negotiations

When an acceptable target has been chosen, the SPAC board enters into discussions with a merger agreement objective: primary negotiating objectives include target valuation and minimum capital conditions (Including if, in the case of a high redemption rate, a PIPE will be committed).

The running costs of SPAC during this period are funded by the pre-IPO and IPO contributions of the sponsor.

There are no restrictions on the type of company a SPAC can acquire, though many will highlight a target industry before IPO. The following are two major considerations when approving an SPAC target.

Target Industry

When look for a target company, most SPACs will identify a sector or a specific location. Most SPACs would not, however, be prevented from pursuing companies or assets in any location or sector.

Target Size

As per the rules of the stock exchange, the target firm's fair market value must be 80 percent or more of the trust assets of the SPAC at the time the definitive agreement for the De-SPAC transaction is signed.

When the acquisition is complete, the founders will take advantage of their shareholding in the new company, typically 20% of the common stock, while the shareholders will receive equity interest on the basis of their capital investment.

In the case that the agreed period expires before the completion of the acquisition, the SPAC is terminated and the income from the IPO held in the trust account is returned to the shareholders.

For the De-SPAC transaction, there is no maximum transaction size. However, the arrangement of the trust account of a SPAC is structured to prevent the SPAC from being listed under the Investment Company Act of 1940, as modified (the "Investment Company Act"), as an "investment company."

Most SPAC IPO prospectuses include disclosure to this end, which states that the SPAC IPO "**will only complete a Business Combination if the post-Business Combination company owns or acquires 50% or more of the issued and outstanding voting securities of the target or otherwise acquires a controlling interest in the target business sufficient for it not to be required to register as an investment company under the Investment Company Act**" (SEC, 2020).

Often, this is interpreted by those reading SPAC IPO prospectuses as the target business' maximum size being twice as much as that of the SPAC. However, that interpretation is not right.

The limitation of the Investment Company Act does not indicate that SPAC investors have to own 50 percent of the surviving corporation's voting shares, as the Investment Company Act merely mandates that the public company take control of its operating subsidiaries and is oblivious to how much of the public company the SPAC shareholders constitute.

Target Announcement

SPAC investors vote on the proposed target after a deal is agreed with the chosen target: a clear majority of shareholders is needed for the target to be accepted.

It will also take some time (generally months) to finalize the transaction after the agreement is accepted by the shareholders.

The SPAC will usually need to seek investor approval for a combination once it is established, and will draft and submit a proxy statement (Or a joint proxy and registration statement on Form S-4 if, as part of the combination, it plans to register new stocks).

This document will include numerous topics requiring the approval of shareholders, including a review of the proposed combination and governance issues.

A host of financial details from the target business will also be included, such as past financial reports, analysis and debates of management (MD&A) and pro forma financial reports illustrating the impact of the combination.

Once the SPAC acquisition is approved by shareholders and all legal concerns have been addressed, the combination will close and the target corporation will become a public corporation.

Once accepted, SPAC owners have the right to redeem their shares in the trust account for a pro rata share of the money.

The sponsor will aim to obtain the requisite approvals for the proposed deal once a combination is announced. The combination with the target business is usually referred to as 'de-SPACing'.

How SPACs Target Companies to Acquire

The sponsor will start the quest for a target company to acquire after the SPAC has concluded its IPO. The following are some of the key considerations in choosing a target company.

Deal Size

As per the exchange rules, the business merger must be with one or more targets that have a combined fair market value of at least 80 percent of the assets kept in the trust account of the SPAC.

Therefore, SPACs often choose business merger targets that are four to eight times the SPAC size to alleviate the dilutive effect of the 20 percent founder shares and make a De-SPAC deal more appealing to a target.

Industry

For their target business combinations, most SPACs choose a particular location or sector to focus on.

Upside Potential

Like every other M&A buyer, SPACs aim to merge with targets that the sponsors consider have a major upside.

SPACs have been increasingly concentrating this year on emerging growth firms that are comparatively earlier than conventional IPO firms.

Financial Reports

The proxy rules of the SEC mandate a proxy statement to contain two or three years of target financial reports plus provisional financial reports.

The financial reports and the auditor of the target must meet certain criteria, and therefore the required audit or re-audit of the financial reports of the target may be a key element for the business merger.

PUBLIC COMPANY READINESS

It is critical that the target firm and its financial controls are ready to manage the rigor of becoming a public company with regular reporting requirements.

MARKET OPPORTUNITY

SPACs would typically search for targets that have a wide market potential for their business.

QUALITY MANAGEMENT TEAM

The consistency of the management team of a target would be a major factor for the sponsor.

DUE DILIGENCE

The SPAC, like the due diligence in M&A or IPO transactions, will conduct thorough due diligence on the target business.

The Key Negotiating Issues between SPAC and a Target Company

The following are some of the main issues that can arise in the negotiations between the SPAC and a target company.

Valuation

In a SPAC merger, the evaluation of the target firm is subject to negotiation.

However, since the approval of the SPAC shareholders is required for the merger and SPAC shareholders can choose to redeem their stake in the company, the valuation must be considered by such shareholders as acceptable, or the transaction may result in higher redemptions and thus less operating capital for the go-forward business.

Also, you might not get long-term investors apart from the sponsor. This is because people who invest in SPACs have different objectives than a regular investor.

For instance, they may not know or care about your business until it's time to acquire it.

Some investors may also be cautious about purchasing shares in a business that went public via a SPAC.

This is because the level of due diligence needed for a merger may be lower than what a standard IPO requires, as mandated by the Securities and Exchange Commission. This may make investors skeptical about a company that went public via a SPAC.

Sponsor Equity

Usually, a SPAC sponsor/management team begins with a 20% interest in the SPAC (plus its at-risk equity stake), but is reduced once the business merger is completed.

In certain cases, some of their equity interests could be sacrificed by the SPAC sponsor/management team to further attract the target selling business or an alternative source of funding for the offer.

The SPAC sponsor, for instance, will always agree to revise the proportion of its promotion on the basis of the trading price and the amount of capital generated in the deal.

Deal Certainty

The target company risks losing a great deal of time, money, and legal fees invested in working on a deal with a SPAC if the SPAC investors do not accept it.

In this case, the associated PIPE funding cannot be raised or, more typically, the SPAC investors may redeem a large portion of the funds in the trust account.

Over the prescribed time span (usually two years, with certain extensions of up to 18 months or 3 years), the SPAC may not find an appropriate merger, and investor money would be tied up for that duration.

In the low-interest-rate setting we are presently in, the lost opportunity cost of the resources being tied up has been lowered.

Investors are usually seen to be paid by both the warrants for this opportunity cost and by obtaining optionality on the De-SPAC deal if the stock price trades up on launch.

In any case, the organization looking to go public via a SPAC would be at a loss if a suitable target firm isn't found within the specified timeframe.

Employee Incentives

Before a business combination, it is important to consider the structure of incentives for employees and management.

It is also important to consider if the stock of the target company will be assumed by the SPAC.

Moreover, it is critical to ascertain if a new equity plan will be adopted on a go-forward basis.

Finally, you need to know if there is intensified vesting of any or all of the target corporation's outstanding stock options to benefit option holders.

Target Quality

Most SPACs have traditionally searched out businesses with positive EBITDA. However, some recent high-profile acquisitions included pre-revenue businesses with enticing investment ideas.

Although the landscape of SPACs in 2020 is very different from what it was decades earlier, historically, the returns for SPACs with closed business mergers have been much worse than conventional IPOs.

Some investors may believe that SPAC targets have been inappropriately screened or have not been able to gather investment bank backing for an offering.

To counter this assumption, management should do everything possible to ensure perfect financial statements and internal controls.

The most serious risk associated with the SPAC structure is that the company would spend the time and resources needed to produce audited financials and the requisite disclosure documentation only for the deal to fall through.

Reason for failure could be the deal being voted against by a large number of shares. Or even if the deal goes through, cash redemptions may surpass the minimum required by the corporation.

Although the volume of SPAC liquidations has been low in recent times, more deals may fail due to a market downturn. This makes it even more critical to ensure the quality of the target company and prove it to investors.

Paperwork

If you are searching for a strategic partner but don't want to manage the troubles and time commitments of a conventional IPO, being bought by or merging with a SPAC is a great option.

That said, it is essential to recognize that an S-4, which contains the specifics of a merger or acquisition, would still have to be filed with the U.S. Commission for Securities and Exchange (SEC).

Many of the specifications, such as filing an S-1 to list the securities with the SEC, are identical to a typical IPO as well.

If the appropriate paperwork is not completed or improperly submitted, businesses may experience regulatory snags that stall the transaction and distract managers from key business efforts.

Additionally, due to the lack of sufficient internal controls or SEC-mandated financial reports, a target company could simply not be ready for a public company.

In consultation with the target business auditors, this is a crucial problem to be rooted out early on.

REPS AND WARRANTIES

A variety of declarations and warranties regarding its creation, good standing, financial reports, debts, intellectual property, critical contracts, and a range of other things would be expected from both the SPAC and the target entity.

Closing Conditions

What are the SPAC business merger's core closing conditions? Typical requirements include the approval of shareholders, no significant adverse impact on the aim and any necessary regulatory approvals.

Moreover, most deals contain a minimum cash requirement in favor of the target if the deal does not collect a threshold amount of money.

Also, there may be further SPAC risks that arise following a closed deal, depending on your business. For instance, in the sense that a sale to SPAC would not indicate a "complete" exit, there are unique considerations for private equity-backed businesses.

As investors look to optimize their returns by secondary sales after the merger, this may cause some nuance.

In order to help both parties understand their choices and maximize results for those concerned, a third party may also play a valuable role.

In addition, if the transaction takes the business into new markets or needs other big changes, refining procedures would help you move forward quickly and efficiently.

This is especially true at a time when previously private corporations are adjusting to the oversight that is part of the requirements for disclosure for public companies.

What Happens after the Business Combination with the Target is Complete

The acquisition is effective at this stage and the corporation must comply with all reporting requirements for public corporations under the Stock Exchange Act of 1934 and subsequent regulations.

For any private corporation, the transformation is a major one, requiring strengthened governance, controls, infrastructure, and operating processes.

However, just because the transaction is completed does not necessarily indicate that the stock of the new firm would skyrocket.

That can certainly occur, but as quickly as it can go up, the stock could also go down.

The market action frequently depends on the enthusiasm created by the new combination and, of course, the newly merged corporation's quality and output.

If the stock of the new business increases for a specific number of days beyond a certain level (the exact price is specified in the prospectus but is typically $18), the firm may leverage the warrants to be redeemed.

That implies that a particular date is presented to warrant holders before which they have to take one of the following actions.

They either have to utilize their warrants (i.e. change them to shares), trade them, or otherwise the warrants become useless.

Importance of Target Company and Target Related Information in Determining D&O Insurance

Insurance underwriters would like to see a connection between the skills of the sponsor team and the identified category of potential businesses to acquire.

A board of individuals with a track history of investing in and running similar companies planning to do businesses in the same area would be treated favorably.

However, a team with relevant sector expertise that, for some reason, wants to invest resources in any other industry would be seen more negatively.

In addition to the above, D&O insurance carriers favor writing policies in regions and states where they know the laws of the state, corporate security laws and the landscape of the consumer economy.

Different insurers have stringent rules that stop them from covering regions where they do not have this knowledge and insight.

SPACs targeting companies in the United States, for instance, will find things less challenging with insurance underwriters than those trying to target companies in China.

In addition, certain domestic insurers can only write D&O policies for firms based in the United States.

Lastly, the underwriters try to predict where the cash injection into the SPAC will ultimately be utilized in a transaction when reviewing the S-1

The more precise the details on the target business class and its location presented in the S-1 registration statement, the more confident the insurance underwriters are likely to be regarding the reliability of the information provided.

Therefore, underwriters would be more secure in their ability to interpret the reach of a SPAC's future acquisitions involving a "SaaS tech firm based in North America" as opposed to if the target description simply read "a tech firm without a worldwide location preference."

Being more precise about the target business class provides insurance underwriters with the ability to supply their rating system with extra credits.

This is everything that SPACs wanting to go public via an IPO need to know regarding the target company to merge with. One of the most important steps that come after target search, negotiation, and acquisition is De-SPACing.

In the next chapter, we discuss everything there is to know about De-SPACing.

.

.

Chapter 12: De-SPAC Process

If the sponsor succeeds in finding and acquiring a target company, it would be integrated with the SPAC into a single, publicly traded business combination. This is referred to as a De-SPAC deal or De-SPACing.

In compliance with SEC legislation, the De-SPACing process mandates the buyer to receive shareholder approval.

The new business would then be subjected to a public company's typical criteria.

Although these laws are more nuanced than can be discussed in depth here, the procedure usually involves the commitment to the purchase of the founders' stock, a redemption deal by which SPAC investors can redeem their stock, and the submission of Form 8-K, which is essentially a transaction registration statement

It includes information to be provided in a Form 10 or General Securities Registration Form, which records stocks for trading on U.S. exchanges.

Since any shareholder may elect not to take part in the SPAC deal, the sponsor doesn't always know for certain what proportion of the trust assets will be required to complete the transaction.

As a result, sponsors are typically expected to enter into forward purchasing deals with some of the early investors to provide additional funding for a deal.

Moreover, via a private investment in a public equity (PIPE) deal, the sponsor can generate additional money.

De-SPACing Process

The De-SPAC process starts once a target firm is identified for acquisition. The process of De-SPAC is close to that of the merger of a public corporation.

Under the SEC proxy rule, in the case of this deal, the SPAC serves as the purchaser and needs the authorization of its shareholder.

More than 20 percent of voting stock acceptance is necessary for most SPACs.

The process involves having shareholder meetings and discussions, completing proxy statements, obtaining SEC reports, and eventually getting a definitive merger agreement.

This process will take anywhere from 3 to 5 months, making it the longest step in a SPAC's lifetime.

After deciding on the terms of the acquisition or of the merger, the sponsors must propose the acquisition target to shareholders.

If the sponsor succeeds in finding and acquiring a target company, it would be integrated with the SPAC into a single, publicly traded business combination in what is referred to as a de-SPAC deal.

In compliance with SEC legislation, the de-SPACing process mandates the buyer to receive shareholder approval.

The new business would then be subjected to a public company's typical criteria.

The procedure usually involves the commitment to the purchase of the founders' stock, a redemption deal by which SPAC investors can redeem their stock, and the submission of Form 8-K, which is essentially a transaction registration statement

It includes information to be provided in a Form 10 or General Securities Registration Form, which records stocks for trading on U.S. exchanges. The securities laws considerations for De-SPACing are discussed in detail later.

Since any shareholder may elect not to take part in the SPAC deal, the sponsor doesn't always know for certain what proportion of the trust assets will be required to complete the transaction.

As a result, sponsors are typically expected to enter into forward purchasing deals with some of the early investors to provide additional funding for a deal.

Moreover, via a private investment in a public equity (PIPE) deal, the sponsor can generate additional money.

PIPE

A PIPE is a tool for SPACs to collect additional money from private investors to acquire the target business in the case of a SPAC.

Shareholders and SPAC sponsors can negotiate details of the form of shares, volume and price of the offer.

It is normal for PIPE shares to be assigned at a similar price (generally $10) to the SPAC IPO.

PIPEs are also considered to dilute existing SPAC owners, which is why SPACs have warrants for compensating initial investors in some instances.

The target company risks losing a great deal of time, money, and legal fees invested in working on a deal with a SPAC if the SPAC investors do not accept it.

In this case, the associated PIPE funding cannot be raised or, more typically, the SPAC investors may redeem a large portion of the funds in the trust account.

Due to less regulatory oversight from the SEC, this fundraising approach is considered to be more effective than secondary offerings.

PIPEs are also considered to dilute existing SPAC owners, which is why SPACs have warrants for compensating initial investors in some instances.

Usually, PIPE investments supplement the de-SPAC deal, which effectively adds to the SPAC additional equity leverage. The PIPE capital generation from hedge funds and PE businesses, which tag along for the trip, is organized by SPAC sponsors.

Usually, the proportion of PIPE to SPAC capital is between 2:1 and 3:1. This implies that a $400M SPAC will effectively raise an overall transaction size of $1.2-1.6B.

Fees would be around 20 percent of the size of the initial SPAC (not including the PIPE amount), which goes in the form of equity to the SPAC sponsor, essentially suggesting a mixed fee of 5-6% for the firm as a proportion of the overall capital raised, fairly close to the 5-7% for a conventional IPO.

Let's consider a hypothetical transaction with SPAC. Say the capital initially raised by the SPAC is $300 million.

However, the sponsors identified and secured a $1.6 billion pre-money valuation and a $2.3 billion post-money valuation deal with the target firm.

The outcome of this would be the targeting firm raising a total of $700 million.

In order to complete the transaction and launch the De-SPAC process, the SPAC will conduct a PIPE to generate a further $400 million from private investors.

Shareholder Approval

The De-SPAC process like a public company combination, the only difference being that the buyer (the SPAC) is generally required to acquire shareholder approval, which must be acquired as per the SEC proxy rules, while the target business (generally a private company) does not need an SEC compliant proxy procedure.

The SPAC needs shareholder approval to conclude the planned initial business combination after a sponsor has identified a target.

The shareholders have the opportunity to vote on the contemplated transaction, whether acquisition or merger, which gives them some recourse if a sponsor chooses a company they do not like.

While the rules of the stock exchange don't always mandate voting by the SPAC shareholders, the De-SPAC transaction's structure is such that it may mandate a vote.

When more than 20 percent of the SPAC's voting stock is being issued in the De-SPAC transaction, the rules of the stock exchange will necessitate a shareholder vote.

This leads to the majority of the De-SPAC deals needing a public vote of the SPAC's stockholders, which includes the submission of a proxy statement with the SEC, SEC review and feedback, proxy statement mailing to the stockholders of the SPAC and organizing a meeting of the shareholders.

The proxy period lasts three to five or more months from the time a definitive deal for the De-SPAC transaction is agreed.

Founder Vote Requirements

The sponsor and any other owners of founder stocks will generally agree at the point of the IPO to vote any founder shares owned they hold and any shares held publicly, acquired during or after the IPO in lieu of the De-SPAC deal.

Because of this, a minimum 20 percent of the outstanding shares of the SPAC will be committed for voting for the deal. This means that attaining majority vote and approval of the deal would require just 37.5% of the public shares.

Founder Shares Vs. Public Shares

Public shares and founder shares are quite comparable in the sense that they automatically change to public shares on a one-to-one basis during the De-SPAC process.

Public shares, though, are general Class A common stock, whereas Class B or Class F common stock is what the founding shares are classified as.

The founder shares are also provided with provisions for anti-dilution and a redemption exemption.

As stated previously, after a SPAC has an IPO, it has a period of approximately 12-24 months to find a business combination, and till that time, the funds stay in a trust account.

The SPAC moves through what is called a "De-SPAC transaction" until the target company has been announced.

However, some SPACs might require a PIPE in order to conclude the De-SPAC transaction.

Redemption Offer

Once the SPAC acquisition is approved by shareholders and all legal concerns have been addressed, the combination will close and the target corporation will become a public corporation.

Once accepted, SPAC owners have the right to redeem their shares in the trust account for a pro rata share of the money.

After the original business combination, each SPAC investor can either continue being a company shareholder or redeem and collect their pro rata sum of funds kept in the trust account.

As the SPAC transitions from simply a trust account into an operating entity, this is a vital investor factor.

As an investor, you can choose to redeem your stock for a pro rata share of the net sum on investment in the trust account or continue being an investor in the merged company going forward.

You can do the above based on how you see the potential initial business merger and its valuation.

The investor gives up his stake of the SPAC when shares are redeemed. Instead, they earn the equivalent proportional interest in the trust account (generally $10.00 plus the interest on the treasury bonds accrued).

In principle, then, common shares in a SPAC can never sell below $10.00 plus interest.

This is because any lower price will present an incentive for arbitration as the shareholder can always reclaim it before the completion of a merger for a pro rata share of the cash in the trust account

Of course, if shares are trading over $10.00 plus interest, it is recommended that an investor does not redeem their shares and sell them on the stock market instead.

While the sponsors receive 20 percent ownership in the SPAC, this share cannot be used to redeem cash held in trust.

This implies that if the sponsor fails to close a deal, their equity stake will become pointless.

Since investors are willing to redeem shares, sponsors need to track cash closely to make sure that adequate capital is available to obtain the aim and handle post-close operations.

However, the redemption offer does not extend to public warrants or retail investors.

The shell company chooses a start-up to merge with following the IPO and seeks approval from institutional investors. However, there is no involvement of retail investors in the decision.

If the SPAC's selection is accepted, but institutional investors don't like the selection, or they just don't think the share price will grow, they can get all their money reimbursed and no questions will be asked from them.

This promise of "satisfaction guaranteed or reimbursement" does not apply to ordinary or retail investors.

They are allowed to sell their shares, which is a right given to all investors of public stocks.

However, at the same time, share prices may have plummeted, meaning that ordinary or retail investors may lose money on a transaction they didn't have any say in.

There is more. Institutional investors receive warrants as incentives for investing pre-IPO.

Let's suppose they purchased a thousand shares for 12 dollars per share. They may even get warrants to purchase a thousand more at 13 dollars per share.

If the stocks pop to $16, they can enforce their warrants and collect the 60 percent profits not just on their initial investment but also on the additional thousand shares, thus multiplying their profit.

Unfortunately, regular investors don't get to rip open this fun little surprise, as you may have already guessed. There are no warrants for them.

Filing Form 8-K

A Form 8-K must be submitted with the US Securities and Exchange Commission (SEC) within four business days of closure.

The form must include details similar to what would be needed in the Form 10 submission of the target firm (usually referred to as the Super 8-K).

The SPAC will usually file a current Form 8-K filing and release a statement informing investors when separate trading will begin.

Investors buying SPAC stocks on the open exchange after the IPO must know whether they are buying warrants, common stock, or units.

Usually, the IPO statement of registration a SPAC would state that the SPAC will submit such a Form 8-K immediately after the IPO is consummated.

If an overallotment option is exercised after the submission of this Form 8-K, a separate Form 8-K with a revised audited balance sheet must be submitted.

The balance sheet to be submitted by the SPAC needs to show the overallotment exercise.

Usually, the underwriting agreement also includes covenants that enable

Many of the details in the Super 8-K will already be contained in the proxy statement or tender offer documents of the SPAC for the De-SPAC deal. Still, extra financial reporting data for the target company might be needed for the Super 8-K.

SPACs are "shell companies" as per the Securities Act of 1933, as revised (the "Securities Act"), as registrants with properties composed entirely of cash and cash equivalents, and the relevant laws and forms.

SEC regulations forbid or restrict the use of a range of waivers, safe harbors and forms allocated to other registrants by shell corporations (SPACs) and previously shell corporations (former SPACs).

In 2005, due to the supposed use of some shell corporations as mediums to perpetrate fraud and abuse the SEC's regulations, the SEC introduced some of these limitations. Based on the individual rule, the restrictions apply to SPACs and previously SPACs for different time frames.

For instance, until at least sixty days after filing a Super 8-K, a previously SPAC is not entitled to file securities offerings under employee benefits on Form S-8.

Moreover, stockholders of previous SPACs are mandated for a duration of 12 months from the date of submission of the Super 8-K to retain their equity before being able to depend on Rule 144 under the Securities Act.

Rule 144 offers a way for individuals who would otherwise be called 'statutory underwriters' (and who are thus mandated to register their equity offer under the Securities Act before their public sale) to trade their equity without registering, normally after a six-month holding period.

Furthermore, SPACs and previously SPACs (i) are not qualified to be well-known experienced issuers until at least three years following the De-SPAC deal, (ii) are restricted in their right to provide reference details on Form S-1 in long-form statements of registration, and (iii) are not entitled to use the "Baby Shelf Rule" for 12 months after the submission of the Super 8-K form.

Deal Size

As per the exchange rules, the business merger must be with one or more targets that have a combined fair market value of at least 80 percent of the assets kept in the trust account of the SPAC.

Therefore, SPACs often choose business merger targets that are four to eight times the SPAC size to alleviate the dilutive effect of the 20 percent founder shares and make a De-SPAC deal more appealing to a target.

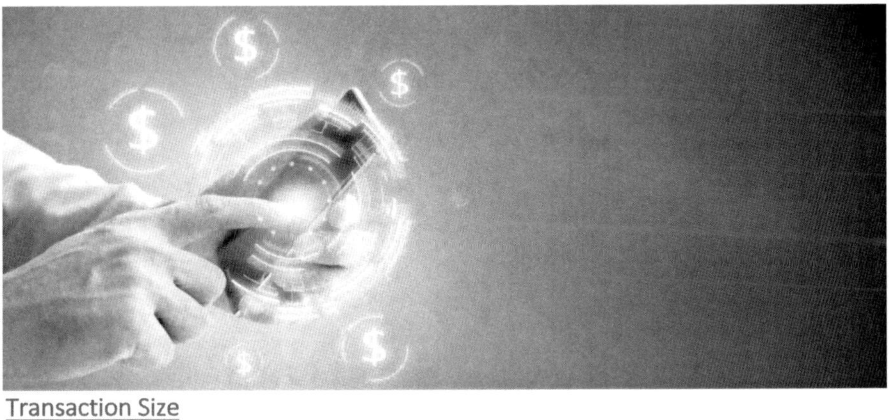

Transaction Size

For the De-SPAC transaction, there is no maximum transaction size. However, the arrangement of the trust account of a SPAC is structured to prevent the SPAC from being listed under the Investment Company Act of 1940 as an "investment company."

Most SPAC IPO prospectuses include disclosure to this end, which states that the SPAC IPO "**will only complete a Business Combination if the post-Business Combination company owns or acquires 50% or more of the issued and outstanding voting securities of the target or otherwise acquires a controlling interest in the target business sufficient for it not to be required to register as an investment company under the Investment Company Act**" (SEC, 2020).

De-SPACing Process from a Reporting Standpoint

The de-SPACing process begins from the reporting point of view and the new company formally begins its life as a public corporation post-business merger by submitting the so-called "Form 10" details

Recently de-SPACed corporations are generally willing to offer incentives to participants of the board of directors and management team of the new firm after the conclusion of the SPAC business combination and the submission of the Form 10 details and as part of the start of their new existence as a public corporation.

As for other public corporations, these awards are usually carried out under an equity reward or equivalent award scheme and are listed with the SEC on Form S-8.

Form S-8 is one of the most simple SEC statements of registration for most firms since it can be used to register stocks to be sold to the employees of the company under any employee benefits package and is eligible for re-offers and resales of both stocks held by business affiliates and limited securities, according to specific rules and restrictions.

Form S-8 is not checked by the SEC; additionally, it is considered instantly effective upon submission and is relatively easy and inexpensive to use. However, Form S-8 poses some unique challenges for previously SPACs.

As the previously SPAC resumes its existence as a public corporation, investors, workers, associates and those who own "restricted stocks" or "control stocks" in the firm and are eager to sell those stocks and/or shift them to their fund manager or other investment accounts will inevitably make inquiries from it and are eager to sell those securities and/or shifting them to their fund manager or other investment accounts

In certain cases, about six months after the de-SPACing activity, the first of these probes occur and take the shape of company security holders demanding that the firm or its transfer agent lift the limiting legends on their stocks.

As the reason for their application, most of these holders may reference Rule 144.

Because of the evergreen requirement of Rule 144 and the inaccessibility of Rule 144 for twelve months after the submission of Form 10 details, resale statements of registration and the privileges to such statements of registration frequently form a crucial part of the business merger negotiations after the conclusion of the merger.

Additionally, owing to the SEC's recent CD&I on S-3 eligibility for previously SPACs, they are expected to have an even greater impact.

Traditionally, in the first weeks or months after de-SPACing, many previously SPACs have found themselves confronting resale statement of registration requirements, although this could change in the future.

Only lawyers who are skilled in the specifics and SPAC-specific challenges placed by U.S. securities regulations are likely to understand and answer these issues at the time of negotiating registry privileges for a SPAC.

On a side note, many previously SPACs remain highly acquisitive or otherwise engaged public corporations, particularly those that have completed a de-SPACing activity in recent times.

Because of this, many of these firms are returning to the public securities markets for purchase funding, general funds generation or other dealings carried out under the SEC registration system, many of which are likely to be affected by the recent guidelines and restrictions of the SEC on the use of Form S-3.

In addition, businesses often use "free writing prospectuses" ("FWPs") or written instructions that represent an offer to sell or an adjuration of an offer to purchase registered stocks and are not a formal prospectus pursuant to Section 10 of the Securities Act of 1933, as modified (the "Securities Act"), in the form of underwritten public offerings.

FWPs may take the shape of written documents, radio or television transmissions, or electronic graphic media, which may include, as submitted with the SEC, information not found in the company statement of registration.

Businesses widely use FWPs for their great versatility in transmitting information to the public. FWPs cannot, however, be used by firms that are' ineligible issuers.' The following are some important pieces of information to know during and after the De-SPACing process.

Form 10 Information

It refers to the standard that, after the business merger agreement, public entities must furnish robust market reports, similar to those mandated by the statements of registration on Form S-1; it comprises of financial reports and summary reports on the firm, its management, and its shares.

This condition is often satisfied by recently de-SPACed firms through the submission by such firms of a Current Report on Form 8-K that contains the Form 10 details (a "Super 8-K").

As the firm continues to exist as a public entity, several securities law constraints and responsibilities related to it, as a former SPAC, are linked to the timing of the submission of Form 10 details.

Shell Company Status

Although often considered synonymous with the procedure of SPAC and de-SPACing, it refers to the day on which the business stopped to be a shell company.

This date is normally a few days before the date on which the Form 10 details on the Super 8-K is filed and is the date on which the business merger transaction closes.

FORM S-8

It is only accessible to former shell corporations (including SPACs) if: (i) the firm has not been a shell company for a minimum of 60 days before the submission of the S-8 statement of registration; and (ii) the firm has submitted a minimum sixty calendar days before the submission of the S-8 with the SEC current Form 10 records, indicating its status as an entity other than a shell corporation.

In general, these provisions lead to a 60-day delay between the closure of the business merger and the submission of Form 10 details for the former SPAC and the right of the SPAC to submit an S-8 statement of registration, including grants under a new merged company incentive scheme.

In several cases, because of the need to file the appropriate grants with the SEC, this causes a considerable delay in the company making such reward grants to its officers and directors.

RULE 144

It provides a waiver from registration for certain resales of limited or regulated securities, subject to the fulfillment of several conditions, including the retention period for the related securities and, in some cases, limitations on the amount and nature of sales.

Rule 144 enforces specific requirements for previously shell corporations, including SPACs, that requires that the company: (i) stopped to be a 'shell corporation' as specified in the rule; (ii) is an SEC reporting firm; (iii) has submitted all the reports that needed to be submitted with the SEC in the previous twelve months; and (iv) has submitted current Form 10 details with the SEC, indicating that the firm is no longer a shell corporation and that a minimum of one year has passed since that Form 10 information was submitted.

The above mentioned condition for current SEC disclosure is known as the "evergreen provision." The outcome of the evergreen clause is that the existing reporting requirement of the Exchange Act for previously SPACs is permanent.

As a consequence, despite investors having fulfilled the holding period and other conditions to sell the stocks of the previously SPAC under Rule 144, no sales will take place unless the firm is current in the disclosure of its Exchange Act.

If the company fails to file a requested Exchange Act covered by the provisions of the regulation, it will stop being current in its records on the Exchange Act and will not comply with this provision for the use of Rule 144.

The further consequence of this evergreen clause is, in most cases, the restrictive legend present on "restricted stocks" of the previously SPAC cannot be withdrawn in advance of a transaction.

This can be troublesome and frustrating for SPAC shareholders, as it can affect everything from the distribution and retention in brokerage accounts of the concerned company's shares to the administration and productivity of future sales.

S-3 ELIGIBILITY

Former SPACs are a critical concern, primarily due to the restrictions faced by SPACs on the use of Rule 144 and the qualification dilemma is likely to present difficulties in securing registration rights in SPAC transactions in the future.

The SEC released new guidelines on September 21, 2020, restricting the ability of former SPACs to fulfill the eligibility criteria of Form S-3. The instruction of the employees seems to restrict the right of the previously SPAC to use Form S-3 during the twelve calendar months after the conclusion of the SPAC business merger deal.

For a previously SPAC, the main issue is whether it is appropriate to use the pre-business merger SEC disclosure record of the SPAC to determine S-3 qualification after the business merger.

The SEC staff reported in the September CD&I that a former SPAC does not use Form S-3 in circumstances where a post business merger firm is a "new entity" or "successor registrant" of the SPAC.

In each of these situations, the CD&I stipulates that for 12 months after the business merger, the corporation will not be able to use Form S-3.

Furthermore, the SEC's guidelines suggest that, in situations where the post-merger corporation is not a new entity nor a replacement for the SPAC, the entity will have a post-merger disclosure record of fewer than 12 months. Thus the SEC staff would be unlikely to improve the efficacy of the statement of registration on Form S-3.

In the absence of further clarity or justification, the outcome of this latest guidance tends to be that most previously SPACs should anticipate Form S-3 to be unavailable for twelve months after the conclusion of the business merger.

This is likely to have a major effect on SPACs in the future, as they and the private operating companies they are trying to merge with will have to deal with and cope with the rising costs and time needed for the first year after the business merger agreement using Form S-1.

Ineligible Users

As specified in Securities Act's Rule 405, these refer to issuers that are or, for the previous 3 years, have been blank check firms.

This comprises SPACs and, thus, previously SPACs, for a duration of three years from the conclusion of the de-SPACing process, are considered disqualified issuers.

Ineligible issuer classification prevents the use of FWPs during this time period.

This, together with the problems pertaining to S-3 eligibility for previously SPACs, can lead to a more rigorous, more stringent and less fluid potential for capital generation in the early years after de-SPACing via the SEC registration process and may compel the affected companies to consider alternative approaches and/or spend additional time and resources to resolve these problems.

We have now covered almost everything there is to know about creating an SPAC and talking an SPAC public via an IPO.

Using this knowledge, we can now compare SPAC with traditional IPO to determine which is better.

In the next chapter, we compare SPAC with traditional IPO to see which option is better for companies looking to go public.

Chapter 13: SPAC vs Traditional IPO

Certain market participants believe that, through a SPAC transaction, a private company can become a publicly traded company with more certainty about pricing and control over deal terms than traditional initial public offerings (IPOs).

These types of transactions, most commonly where a SPAC acquires or merges with a private company, often occur many months or more than a year after the SPAC has completed its own IPO.

Unlike an operating company that becomes public through a traditional IPO, however, a SPAC is a shell company when it becomes public. This means that it does not have an underlying operating business and does not have assets other than cash and limited investments, including the proceeds from the IPO.

A SPAC's most significant benefit compared to a traditional IPO is the time it takes between planning to go public and actually becoming a publicly traded company.

No organization wants to spend 12 to 18 months corresponding with the underwriters and the SEC, followed by a pre-IPO roadshow.

SPACs provide businesses with an opportunity to go public in just 4-6 months, allowing additional time for the team to concentrate on developing the company and growing shareholder value.

Since SPACs can abstract the IPO process, a private firm can merge into an already publicly traded (blank shell) corporation with substantially less work than required by a traditional IPO.

For the SPAC IPO, SEC registration documents are brief and can be completed within a few weeks. Historical financial reports or properties that need to be disclosed are not needed.

In addition, the SPAC sponsors spend the coming months on roadshows to generate money.

SPACs assume all IPO activity on the boilerplate, allowing the target organization to discuss just conditions, terms, and other regular M&A processes.

Not only is merging with a SPAC a faster way to go public than direct listing or a traditional IPO, but it also relieves you from the responsibilities of a roadshow.

This is because a roadshow is not a requirement with a SPAC. There's no need to sell yourself and gain the attention of investors.

This is great news considering travel, in-person meetings, activities, and other discussions are more regulated and can introduce new risks.

Therefore, acquiring a SPAC is a saner operation that generates less urgent and prolonged scrutiny.

And since a roadshow is not required, the SPAC will spend more time concentrating on priorities such as your business, providing greater emphasis and reducing the time needed to obtain access to public markets.

How A SPAC Differs from a Traditional IPO

A SPAC can be seen as the opposite of a conventional IPO. A SPAC first goes public, typically with a highly respected management team capable of raising capital from large institutional investors, with the goal of purchasing a private firm within around 24 months to place it in its shell.

An IPO is essentially a money-seeking business, whereas a SPAC is a business seeking money. Going public via a SPAC will speed up the market entry of a business by anywhere from two to four months.

Considering the lack of financial reports and related materials, there are fewer SEC concerns and queries to answer without a corporation in the actual shell, which shortens the auditing process.

Additionally, instead of attempting to sell a business to public investors at a roadshow, a SPAC provides added assurity of getting a long-term investor base through a private-public equity fund, or PIPE, that is in place.

Usually, that kind of assurance is not available in an IPO unless it is perfectly clear that the business will do well.

SPACs are growing in popularity and many companies today prefer to use them instead of traditional IPO to go public.

This is because SPACs offer several benefits not provided by a conventional IPO to sponsor-organizers and businesses that choose to go public. One is the simplified criteria for disclosure that saves trees, funds, and time.

Another possible reason is that, in recent years, there have been instances of businesses taking the conventional IPO route and decreasing in value during the roadshow phase due to investor scrutiny, causing the company to withdraw its IPO filing.

By contrast, the SPAC IPO path entails relatively less investor scrutiny because the entity going public is not really a corporation, so there is not much to scrutinize.

This renders the SPAC IPO more appealing to riskier businesses or businesses in riskier sectors, such as the media industry.

This is particularly true if the current investors in those firms are anxious and looking for the business to sell or go public in order to cash out their shares.

Firms that are "risky enough" that they might not be accepted in the traditional IPO market are those that are likely to opt for a SPAC IPO.

In a SPAC IPO, however, the scrutiny is not actually abolished. Instead, it is redirected and reduced.

The initial investors decide whether to take a gamble on the sponsor and acquisition strategy of the SPAC, knowing that if a majority disagrees with the ultimate acquisition target, they will have their money refunded.

Therefore, the acquisition could be more scrutinized by investors than the IPO. On the other hand, they (the investors) have already endorsed the sponsor championing the acquisition.

Therefore, the investors are likely to go along with the transaction unless the sponsor really goes off track with the acquisition target.

The involvement of fewer individuals is another reason SPAC IPOs are so popular.

A traditional IPO involves many investors negotiating concurrently with issuers and underwriters on particular terms such as underwriter rights, executive pay, the offer price, and several other issues.

However, in a SPAC, it is generally just the target company and the sponsor that are involved in the negotiations. This helps to speed up the process.

Costs of SPAC vs. Traditional IPO

While expenses for a SPAC do not differ too much from expenditures for a traditional IPO, the arrangement of discounts for underwriters and the overall underwriting process can be more advantageous for a business looking to go public.

One or more investment banks that earn an underwriting concession as an incentive to promote and sell the IPO can be underwriters of a traditional IPO.

The discount for traditional IPO underwriters is generally about 3.5-7 percent, as per PWC.

On the other hand, the SPAC IPO's underwriting concession is 5.5%, with 2% payment during the IPO and the remainder 3.5% payment at the time of the de-SPAC transaction.

In addition, the underwriting discount payment is usually made as equity options in the business to the SPAC sponsors.

The delayed discount commission helps the target organization and positively influences sponsors to identify a target acquisition to earn their 3.5 percent commission as equity.

To say it another way, instead of paying the SPAC sponsors in the form of equity, the payment that a corporation would make to an investment bank to underwrite an IPO is instead made to the SPAC sponsors.

A lock-up arrangement for 180 days from the pricing of the IPO is signed by the officers, directors, and sponsors in a traditional IPO.

The standard lock-up for a SPAC IPO lasts for up to one year from the closure of the De-SPAC deal, subject to early removal if the common shares are trading over a fixed price (typically $12.00 per share) for twenty out of thirty trading days beginning 150 days after the De-SPAC deal is completed.

Although the cost of going public could be more or less the same, in comparison to a conventional IPO, benefits for underwriters and the business are more integrated into the SPAC process.

PRICING AND VALUATION IN SPAC VS. TRADITIONAL IPO

SPACs offer the sponsors (underwriters) a stronger incentive structure for the target business to collect capital on favorable terms than a traditional IPO.

Investment banks that underwrite the traditional IPO do not have the same motivations as the business.

Banks want to retain their sales relationships and sell shares in firms that are likely to make the most money for their clients.

Examples of the mismatch of rewards between banks and the long-term performance of a pre-IPO business are Greenshoe options and over-allotment options.

It is not unusual for a corporation's stocks, also known as "pop," to trade higher than the IPO price when they're first listed on an exchange.

In a traditional IPO, Banks ignore the corporation's concerns and inappropriately price the IPO to make a pop to reward early investors (clients of the bank) who assume more risk.

A big pop encourages banks to sell more shares to stabilize the price, a mechanism referred to as over-allotment. In this case, because they have earned capital at a much lower valuation, the business leaves money on the table.

On the other hand, when there is no pop and the stock trades slightly lower than the IPO price, the option for underwriters to buy back shares is provided by a lack of supply to push the price back up.

This is the greenshoe alternative, which is typically written during the phase of underwriting.

The above options allow banks to monitor the IPO process to minimize drawbacks for themselves and their clients.

As the sponsors are basically the underwriters of a SPAC, they ultimately have the same long-term benefits as the corporation. It can be viewed as an M&A approach rather than a transaction.

While negotiations can be complicated, they're all on the same page until the merger is accomplished.

In addition, when they are positive about a target firm, sponsors of the SPAC place their credibility on the line. This generally results in the firm's fair and favorable valuation.

SPAC INVESTMENT VS. IPO

A SPAC is a shell corporation when it becomes public. This is different from an operating company that becomes public through a traditional IPO.

This implies that the SPAC does not have an existing operating business and has no assets other than cash and small investments, including IPO revenues.

You depend on the management team that established the SPAC, often alluded to as the sponsor(s), if you invest in a SPAC at the IPO level, as the SPAC seeks to acquire or merge with an existing company.

This merger or acquisition is referred to as the initial business combination.

A SPAC may specify a particular industry or sector in its IPO prospectus that it will pursue as it tries to merge with an operating company, but it is not obliged to look for a target in the sector specified.

Once the SPAC has established an initial business merger opportunity, its leadership enters the discussion with the operating company and performs the business combination if accepted by the SPAC shareholders (if an investor vote is needed).

This deal is typically organized as a reverse merger in which the operating company combines with the SPAC or a division of the SPAC and merges therein.

Although the original business merger can be organized in different ways, after the deal, the merged entity is a publicly traded company. It takes on the business of the target operating company.

DIFFERENCE IN TRADING PRICE

Generally, SPACs are priced at a modest $10 per unit in the IPO. The SPAC IPO price is not dependent on the value of an established corporation, unlike the traditional IPO of an operating company.

When the warrants, common stock, and units start trading, their market values will fluctuate and there may be no connection between these variations and the SPAC's ultimate financial performance.

IPO WINDOW DIFFERENCE

Timing is the most important thing in a traditional IPO and missing the appropriate "window" may be the difference between a good "pop" and a poor IPO-at least by certain standards.

On the other hand, the very concept of a SPAC fits well with the somewhat shut IPO window.

The SPAC market is most active and could be even more so when economic uncertainty or macro shocks shut the IPO window.

The risks of not raising the capital via institutional investors or adjusting the price of the offer are all avoided as these are accomplished when the money for the SPAC is generated and put in the investment fund for holding. This has been done many times already.

NO TRUST ACCOUNT IN TRADITIONAL IPO

Usually, SPAC IPO revenues minus revenue used for some fees and costs are kept in a trust account. This is not seen with a traditional IPO.

A third party holds the money before the deal is finalized, equivalent to an escrow agreement when purchasing a property—in the case of a SPAC, the original business combination—or the SPAC is liquidated for not having concluded an initial business combination within a specified time period.

In general, SPACs invest the revenues in reasonably secure, interest-bearing investment vehicles.

However, the precise terms of the offer should be closely checked because there is no law requiring the revenues to be invested only in certain types of vehicles.

SPACs typically use the interest on trust account investments to pay taxes.

A SPAC gives its investors the ability to redeem their holdings connected with a corporate merger rather than simply being a shareholder in the merged entity.

If the SPAC does not complete a business merger, the investors shall be beneficiaries of the trust and shall have the right to their pro rata share of the net balance upon investment in the trust account.

One thing to remember is that you are only eligible for the pro rata share of the trust account if you bought the stock on the open market and not the rate at which you acquired the SPAC shares on the exchange.

For instance, if a SPAC conducted an IPO at $15 per share, but you acquired 100 SPAC shares at $16 per share on the open market, the stocks you buy are connected to a trust account balance of approximately $15 per share.

So your trust account share will be worth around $1500, rather than the $1600 you've paid for your stock.

To be clear about the conditions of the trust account, particularly your redemption privileges and the scenarios in which cash can be freed from the account, you should carefully read the SPAC IPO prospectus.

DIFFERENCE IN UNDERWRITING DISCOUNT STRUCTURE

SPAC IPOs have a unique underwriting discount model. The underwriters usually earn a concession of 5%-7% of the gross IPO revenues in a traditional IPO, which they deduct from the revenues provided at closing.

The standard discount arrangement in a SPAC IPO is for 2% of the gross revenues to be paid at the closing of the IPO, with another 3.5% being credited into the trust account and due to the underwriters at the close of the De-SPAC deal.

The deferred 3.5 percent discount is never provided to the underwriters if no De-SPAC transaction takes place and is used with the remainder of the trust account balance to reimburse the public shares.

A lock-up arrangement for 180 days from the pricing of the IPO is signed by the officers, directors, and sponsors in a conventional IPO.

The standard lock-up for a SPAC IPO lasts for up to one year from the closure of the De-SPAC deal, subject to early removal if the common shares are trading over a fixed price (typically $12.00 per share) for twenty out of thirty trading days beginning 150 days after the De-SPAC deal is completed.

SPAC Structure vs. Traditional IPO

The SPAC structure offers benefits for the target business and its owners, IPO investors, and SPAC founders.

The SPAC structure allows the target business and its owners to go public during times when the market is unstable.

Other advantages of the SPAC structure the target business and its owners include:

- Access to public markets
- Existing owners' ability to share meaningfully in future growth through stock rollover that is not available in exit through sale
- Access to public capital to finance growth or operations
- Ability to include financial projections in the proxy statement for approval of business combination that is not available in traditional IPO
- Ability to structure a transaction, including cash-out to existing owners and earn-outs that are not available in traditional IPO

The benefits of the SPAC structure for IPO investors include the chance to co-invest with successful founders, downside protection until completion of a business combination, and investment liquidity.

Finally, the benefits of the SPAC structure for IPO founders include a broader potential investors base and greater ease in capital raising compared to private vehicles.

Additionally, they are provided with a platform to monetize proprietary deal flow and have access to a potentially extremely attractive upside and possible serial SPACs.

Difference in Timing of SPAC vs. Traditional IPO

SPAC IPOs can be substantially faster as compared to traditional IPOs. Both financial reports and prospectuses submitted during a SPAC IPO are considerably shorter due to their lack of basic operation and can be assembled in a matter of weeks (unlike the months it takes with a traditional IPO).

There are no past financial statements to be reported or any assets that need an explanation, and there are limited business risk factors.

Consequently, there are generally few comments from the SEC, and there is usually no need for cumbersome adjustments.

The whole SPAC IPO process can be completed from its initiation in as little as fifteen weeks.

The De-SPAC transaction, on the other hand, includes many of the same criteria as would apply to the target firm's IPO, including audited financial reports and other reporting items that may not otherwise apply if a public entity has acquired the target firm.

SPAC Risk vs. Traditional IPO

Although some D&O insurance underwriters currently see SPACs as less risky than the traditional IPO firm, a few others do not hold the same viewpoint.

Also, D&O insurance carriers follow the environment closely to write business in the industry.

Nevertheless, amid already high rates, many carriers claim that the price of D&O insurance for SPAC IPOs continues to be underpriced.

These carriers can only start writing policies if they are willing to charge even higher rates and withholdings.

This is something that some SPACs will need to consider in the future if capacity becomes any more limited than it is now.

Despite the risks and complexities associated with some SPACs that may cause underwriters to come up with a higher fee for D &O insurance, SPACs are seen as an attractive investment.

	SPAC Merger	Traditional IPO
Timing	3-4 Months	6-9 Months
Process	• Limited interruption to management, owner, and employee • Due diligence required but executed by a small dedicated team • SEC review process can be deferred until after the closing	• Comprehensive preparation involving whole organization • Dealing early with analyst/market participants • Full SEC review process
Pricing	• Certainty on price early in the process • Limited risk from fluctuating market conditions	• Price determined at the time of the IPO • Full market risk

Costs	• Lower direct expenses and indirect costs • Typical underwriter fees: 5.5%	• Full range of direct expenses and indirect costs • Typical underwriter fees: 6.0%
Other	• Dedicated experienced and proven senior management • Provide stamp of approval and potential supplement of management	• Potential lack of capital market experience, international and well-known management • Risk of IPO being rescheduled due to underwriter queue

As seen above, there are many differences between a Special Purpose Acquisition Company (SPAC) used to take a company public and a traditional IPO.

In several aspects, a SPAC has the advantage over the traditional IPO, making it a more viable option for taking a company public in most cases.

In addition to knowing the difference between a SPAC and a traditional IPO, it is also important to distinguish between a SPAC and a SHELL. This is done next.

Chapter 14: SPAC vs. SHELL

The Securities & Exchange Commission defines SPAC as a type of Blank Check Company. SPACs have become a popular vehicle for various transactions, including transitioning a company from a private company to a publicly traded company

These types of transactions, most commonly where a SPAC acquires or merges with a private company, often occur many months or more than a year after the SPAC has completed its own IPO.

Unlike an operating company that becomes public through a traditional IPO, however, a SPAC is a shell company when it becomes public. This means that it does not have an underlying operating business and does not have assets other than cash and limited investments, including the proceeds from the IPO.

SPAC: Blank Check or SHELL?

SHELL companies and blank checks are essentially similar. However, there are some clear differences that set each one apart.

A start-up venture that has a carefully crafted plan for developing or providing 'something' but currently has no active operations would classify as a shell company if or until it becomes a public and reporting company since it has negligible assets and operations

However, it does not count as a blank check because it has a legitimate business plan.

On the other hand, an inactive business that used to have activities but has a lot of assets (such as trademarks, third-party claims, or perhaps even a substantial carry forward net operating loss) could classify as a blank check (because its real purpose is to combine) but not a shell corporation (since it retains more than nominal/minimal assets).

A start-up that has any operations is not a shell corporation. However, if it only retains nominal assets and activities, it will still be subject to the disclosure provisions after any reverse merger.

Understanding a Blank Check SPAC

A blank check company is a development stage company with no specific business plan or purpose or has indicated its business plan is to engage in a merger or acquisition with an unidentified company or companies, other entity, or person. These companies typically involve speculative investments and often fall within the SEC's definition of "penny stocks" or are considered "microcap stocks."

In addition, a blank check company registering for a securities offering may be subject to additional requirements for the protection of investors, including depositing most of the raised funds in an escrow account until an acquisition is agreed to and requiring shareholder approval of any identified acquisition.

A type of Blank Check Company is a "special purpose acquisition company" or SPAC for short. A SPAC is created specifically to pool funds in order to finance a merger or acquisition opportunity within a set timeframe. The opportunity usually has yet to be identified.

SPACs are non-operating publicly listed entities, established to find and acquire a private company, activating the publicly listed stock of the acquisition target.

SPACs are also referred to as blank check businesses. It is considered a reverse merger whenever a SPAC or other publicly-traded corporation buys a private company. A merger typically occurs when a private corporation makes a public company private.

UNDERSTANDING SPAC AS A SHELL

A SPAC is a public shell corporation established to complete a business merger with a private operating firm within a defined period.

Merging with an already public shell, the private corporation will effectively accomplish an IPO at a lower cost than a conventional IPO with a preserved public shareholder base. It can also provide greater confidence in a deal in difficult times.

The typical IPO process is turned on its head by a SPAC in that the business that originally goes public is not so much a corporation as the expectation of one. In other words, the SPAC is just a shell company that does not own any assets itself.

Investopedia defines a Shell company as "an organization without actual business activities or substantial assets.

A SPAC can be seen as the opposite of a conventional IPO. A SPAC first goes public, typically with a highly respected management team capable of raising capital from large institutional investors, with the goal of purchasing a private firm within around 24 months to place it in its shell.

An IPO is essentially a money-seeking business, whereas a SPAC is a business seeking money. Going public via a SPAC will speed up the market entry of a business by anywhere from two to four months.

Considering the lack of financial reports and related materials, there are fewer SEC concerns and queries to answer without a corporation in the actual shell, which shortens the auditing process.

Additionally, instead of attempting to sell a business to public investors at a roadshow, a SPAC provides added assurity of getting a long-term investor base through a private-public equity fund, or PIPE, that is in place.

Usually, that kind of assurance is not available in an IPO unless it is perfectly clear that the business will do well.

FOUNDERS OF THE SPAC SHELL

Seasoned business executives create a special purpose acquisition company (SPAC); they are optimistic that their credibility and expertise can help them find a successful company to acquire.

Since SPAC is just a shell company, the founders become the selling point when raising money from investors.

The founders provide the business with the starting capital, and they profit from a significant stake in the acquired firm.

When establishing a special purpose acquisition business, the founders typically have an interest in a particular industry.

Availability of Cash

SPACs usually have cash, unlike the majority of non-operational shell companies.

In most situations, the cash would be less than $5 million in a standard SPAC, but the money helps generate instant capital appreciation and valuation for the transaction target.

History of SPAC SHELL

There is no controversy, expense and hassle of cleaning a former shell company because SPACs lack the questionable past of many previously reporting firms in a reverse merger transaction.

Liabilities of SPAC SHELL

Since the SPAC SHELL has not carried out any material activity and has a clean balance sheet, the target company's shareholders usually face no unforeseen liabilities after the transaction concludes.

SPAC SHELL Existing Workforce

Since a SPAC is a shell corporation with no activities, they do not have in-house teams.

For example, most would involve third-party partners to perform these functions. Therefore, between the capacities of your company and the SPAC, there will often be some discrepancy.

In addition, the internal teams do not have the skills required to follow the steps, the nuanced criteria for documentation, or other strategic factors specific to a SPAC being acquired.

Target firms have often disregarded the finance and technical accounting functions needed to manage these transactions.

And several of them may also be unprepared to undertake the comprehensive due diligence procedure that can again divert managers from day-to-day tasks while exposing businesses to unexpected threats if they are not carefully investigated.

SPAC SHELL INELIGIBLE ISSUERS RULING

A SPAC is deemed a "shell company" under Securities Act Rule 4055 even though it is excluded from Securities Rule 419. As such, the following applies to it:

- A SPAC is an "unqualified issuer," as specified in Securities Act Rule 405, and therefore may not use prospectuses for free writing (the roadshow presentations are subject to additional limitations without the use of the free writing prospectus guidelines).
- SPAC securities owners may not depend on Securities Act Rule 144 for the resale of such securities until one year after completion of the SPAC's initial business combination and submission of current Form 10 details to the SPAC (the SPAC must also have submitted the periodic reports needed under Section 13 or Section 15(d) of the Exchange Act (besides the Form 8-K) for the preceding twelve months (or for such a shorter time as to enable the SPAC to submit such reports).
- Until three years have passed since its initial business combination, a SPAC will not become a well-known experienced issuer; and
- Many of the correspondence safe harbours under the Securities Act cannot be used by a SPAC.

Analysis of Safe Harbor

As a shell corporation and an unqualified issuer, SPACs may not depend on the following safe harbors for correspondence:

- Communications over 30 days before a statement of registration is on file—Rule 163A of the Securities Act
- Research report safe harbors - Securities Act Rules 137, 138 and 139

These limitations expire three years after the initial business combination of the SPAC is concluded.

For communications disclosing an offering, a SPAC may depend on Securities Act Rule 134.

Communications that conform to Rule 134 of the Securities Act are not considered to be a' prospectus,' as specified in Section 2(a)(10) of the Securities Act or a prospectus for free writing.

In addition, SPACs can depend on the rules under the Securities Act on "access equals delivery".

IPO FOR SPAC SHELL

As a shell corporation, SPAC IPOs do not have to report past financial statements or explain assets; the IPO phase can thus be completed much faster than conventional operating companies.

The organization will put out an initial public offering (IPO) for investors soon after the SPAC is organized and will explain it in a prospectus.

SPACs are officially formed when their underwriters file Form S-1 with the SEC on behalf of the management team, indicating their plan to conduct an IPO at some future date.

This initial statement of registration is a lengthy document outlining the process of transforming the registered shell with a standard $25,000 investment into a new public entity that will aim to identify a suitable acquisition goal within a limited period of time.

SHELL Company Status

Although often considered synonymous with the procedure of SPAC and de-SPACing, it refers to the day on which the business stopped to be a shell company.

This date is normally a few days before the date on which the Form 10 details on the Super 8-K is filed and is the date on which the business merger transaction closes.

AVAILABILITY OF FORM S-8

Is only accessible to former shell corporations (including SPACs) if:

(i) The firm has not been a shell company for a minimum of 60 days before the submission of the S-8 statement of registration; and

(ii) (ii) The firm has submitted a minimum sixty calendar days before the submission of the S-8 with the SEC current Form 10 records, indicating its status as an entity other than a shell corporation.

RULE 144 REQUIREMENTS RELATED TO SPAC'S SHELL STATUS

Rule 144 a waiver from registration for certain resales of limited or regulated securities, subject to the fulfillment of several conditions, including the retention period for the related securities and, in some cases, limitations on the amount and nature of sales.

Rule 144 enforces specific requirements for previously shell corporations, including SPACs, that requires that the company: (i) stopped to be a 'shell corporation' as specified in the rule; (ii) is an SEC reporting firm; (iii) has submitted all the reports that needed to be submitted with the SEC in the previous twelve months; and (iv) has submitted current Form 10 details with the SEC, indicating that the firm is no longer a shell corporation and that a minimum of one year has passed since that Form 10 information was submitted.

The IPO Process for SPAC Shells

As a shell corporation, SPAC IPOs do not have to report past financial statements or explain assets; the IPO phase can thus be completed much faster than conventional operating companies.

The organization will put out an initial public offering (IPO) for investors soon after the SPAC is organized and will explain it in a prospectus.

SPACs are officially formed when their underwriters file Form S-1 with the SEC on behalf of the management team, indicating their plan to conduct an IPO at some future date.

This initial statement of registration is a lengthy document outlining the process of transforming the registered shell with a standard $25,000 investment into a new public entity that will aim to identify a suitable acquisition goal within a limited period of time.

Form S-1 showcases the new company's funding requirements, the nature of the issuance of securities, reveals the entire subscription agreement, conflicts of interest between the founders of SPAC and potential investors, explains the proposed business and gives the management team's backstory.

Additionally, Form S-1 notifies the creation of escrow accounts where all capital generated during the IPO will be stored, minus administrative costs, specifies how the revenues from this fund would be utilized if the acquisition occurs and if the SPAC is unable to complete the acquisition and needs to liquidate.

Once Form S-1 is approved by the SEC, a series of preparatory steps for an eventual IPO are carried out by the management team and underwriters. Any relevant adjustment to the initial form is immediately reported with the SEC.

Underwriters file the final prospectus, Form 424-B, just before the IPO date, which lists all adjustments that have occurred since the original registration statement.

Filing Super 8-K

SPACs are "shell companies" as per the Securities Act of 1933, as revised (the "Securities Act"), as registrants with properties composed entirely of cash and cash equivalents, and the relevant laws and forms.

SEC regulations forbid or restrict the use of a range of waivers, safe harbors and forms allocated to other registrants by shell corporations (SPACs) and previously shell corporations (former SPACs).

In 2005, due to the supposed use of some shell corporations as mediums to perpetrate fraud and abuse the SEC's regulations, the SEC introduced some of these limitations. Based on the individual rule, the restrictions apply to SPACs and previously SPACs for different time frames.

For instance, until at least sixty days after filing a Super 8-K, a previously SPAC is not entitled to file securities offerings under employee benefits on Form S-8.

Moreover, stockholders of previous SPACs are mandated for a duration of 12 months from the date of submission of the Super 8-K to retain their equity before being able to depend on Rule 144 under the Securities Act.

SPAC Shells in a Nutshell

Can you imagine investing in a company with no business operations whatsoever? Well some investors do just that when they invest into what are referred to as called a special purpose acquisition company or SPAC shells.

Investors literally put their money into a company with no assets whatsoever and that's why it's called a blank cheque company. You would say, why would anyone do this? Well, the SPAC raises money through an initial public offering right. After they raise money, they put it in an interest-bearing account in a trust so they can't touch most of the money that they got from the IPO.

So what will they do with this money? Why would anyone give them money in the IPO? The SPAC is going to look for a company that they want to acquire, and they might be looking at a specific industry. Maybe they want to get into consumer goods and they're trying to acquire a consumer goods company, or maybe they're open to any type of company whatsoever. Still, basically, they are intending to acquire another firm they're going to merge with.

Then you're going to have the combined entity and the SPAC is going to disappear. Typically, they would take the name of the company that they have merged with.

Now, they need to find another company to merge with and there's a time period of, let's say, two years. If they can't find another company to merge with within two years, then they just have to give the money back to the investors. And the investors don't get a hundred percent of what they had invested because there were some costs involved and so forth with the registration process.

So, why would anyone do this? What is the purpose here? Why wouldn't you just go and buy a private company and take it public? Well., the benefit here of this SPAC is that the IPO is easier to do when you have a shell company that doesn't have any historical financial results; they don't have any assets that they need to make disclosures about. It's really easy compared to like if you were to buy a company that had been in business 30 years and had property, plant and equipment, and intangible assets of different kinds.

It is so much easier to go public with this shell company. So, SPAC is just a shell, which makes it easy to public with it. You can then go find a suitable company and merge them together.

The alternative is if you have found a target company that you don't have much prior knowledge about and still select that as the company to merge with.

You found the target company and want to acquire it. Now, you just need to take them public. However, you will need to get and go through all prior financial statements of this target before you can do that.

You will need to look at their assets and make all these disclosures. You don't have to do that with the SPAC because the SPAC is just a shell; it's just there; it's like a like a holding place for what you're ultimately going to acquire.

Here is a real-world example. Suppose there is a company called ABC acquisition Holdings; they raised almost 700 million dollars through an IPO in 2020. So, ABC acquisition Holdings: that is the SPAC and then they had to file because they were going public.

When you go public in the U.S, you have to follow this s-1 registration statement with the SEC. So, this is just the shell. ABC acquisition holdings don't do anything and they mention this in the s-.1. They report having no operating results.

So, they're not going to do anything there until they get the money from the IPO and then they're going to go out and try and merge with another firm.

Now, they don't know what firm they want to merge with; they have no plans or understandings of any prospective targets, so they don't know.

There isn't a specific firm they hope to get the money with. Moreover, they looked at different firms to see ultimately who they're going to merge with.

If they can't find anybody, then they won't merge at all. Now, they were targeting specifically; they wanted an industrial company and they ended up finding this company XYZ Manufacturing Inc., which basically manufactures equipment for data centers.

So, they ended up merging with them. The SPAC shell: ABC acquisition just disappears after the merger. Now, the combined company is called XXX holdings and it begins trading on the New York Stock Exchange in 2021.

Why Shell Companies Are Considered High-Risk

This bit of information is for investors in a SPAC and companies looking to merge with a Shell.

Shell companies is a term that only seems to exist on paper: a mystery or taboo that lawyers and industry professionals only understand while the general public is kept in the dark about their existence

So, what is a shell company? A shell company is an entity with financial assets but no significant business activity and no publicly known directors or owners; shell companies don't create products, hire employees or generate revenue, yet they somehow store money and engage in financial transactions around the world.

Shell companies in some countries may be referred to as international business corporations, personal investment vehicles, phantom firms, mailbox companies, or letterbox companies.

It looks all good so far. However, shell companies can also be used by criminals for illegal purposes such as money laundering and fraud at an individual and enterprise level.

So, why do shell companies hide the identities of their significant controllers and owners? They do it so that they can be set up anonymously letting, businesses and individuals engage in financial dealings without revealing who they really are.

Shell companies are often created in tax havens. Tax havens are countries with few or no taxes on businesses as well as laws against revealing banking information. By starting a shell company in a tax haven, a business can enjoy lower taxes while still have access to foreign markets.

Criminals like to use shell companies. This is because loan funds coming from criminal activity can be laundered by lending money between criminally controlled companies. This seemingly legitimate use of the funds can make it appear that the funds were being properly integrated into the economy; however, the loan is then repaid with interest to avoid suspicion.

In some cases, companies are established and then merged with another firm to create a complex hierarchy of ownership; this helps to conceal criminal ownership and facilitates the transfer of illicit funds between companies muddying any paper trail, fictitious business expenses, or false invoicing.

It is when a criminal enterprise controls legal entities in different jurisdictions, it can employ a laundering technique known as double invoicing.

The way it works is that offshore company orders goods from its subsidiary in another country and the payment is sent in full to the bank account of the subsidiary. However, both companies are owned by the criminal enterprise and the payment for goods is actually repatriation of illicit money where no goods are actually being purchased.

Similarly, when the criminal sells a business, he has a legitimate source of capital that will then integrate into the local economy, buying a company already owned by their own criminal enterprise.

Another laundering technique is to purchase a company already owned by the criminal enterprise; this laundering method is most frequently used to repatriate illicit money that was previously stashed in a foreign tax haven.

Criminal proceeds from offshore are used to buy a company that the criminal enterprise already owns; this way, the criminal successfully returns a large sum of money that has been concealed in another country, paying out fictitious salaries in addition to claiming the proceeds of crime as legitimate business revenue.

Criminally controlled enterprises will pay out salary to fictitious employees or to people use almost as money mules who receive payment as if it was a salary using nominees as owners or directors to distance the company from its criminal connections.

Nominees will be used as company owners, officers, and directors. They will often but not necessarily have no criminal record. Further, companies established by lawyers will often be registered in the lawyer's name are shell companies.

Illegal shell companies in their own right are not illegal and most people use them for legitimate reasons.

Can shell companies be used for criminal reasons other than money laundering? Yes, there are a number of other criminal reasons why wealthy individuals or criminals would want to use a shell company. An example of this is evading taxes. Wealthy individuals may hide money in shell companies to shield it from the taxman engaging in a legal business. This can be activities such as arms or drugs trade, hiding assets from a spouse: hard to believe, but wealthy individuals use this technique to hide assets from their family or spouse.

Here is a recap of what we just learned:

- A Shell company is a company with financial assets but no significant business activity
- Shell companies don't create products hire employees, or generate revenue; instead, they stash money and engage in financial transactions
- Shell companies can be used for illegal purposes like money laundering or legitimate purposes like storing funds in the early stages of a startup

Well, there you have it—why a shell company is considered high risk.

In the next and last chapter of this book, we will look at the process or journey from SPAC to i-SPAC. In other words, we will look at the path taken by a Special Purpose Acquisition Company (SPAC) to become a public entity.

.

Chapter 15: From SPAC to i-SPAC

A SPAC raises capital through an Initial Public Offering (IPO) for the purpose of acquiring an existing operating company.

Then the sponsor completes the normal filings associated with going public through an IPO.

At the time of their IPOs, SPACs have no existing business operations or even stated targets for acquisition.

Because the company doesn't do anything (i.e. it has no operational business), the filing process is fast and easy.

The sponsor then goes on a roadshow, similar to traditional IPOs, to try to find interested investors.

Investors in SPACs can range from well-known institutional investors to private investment funds.

The difference here is that they are selling themselves, their team, their vision and their experience rather than a specific company.

Once the sponsor has attracted enough interest, they sell securities in the company.

The money raised from the IPO is put into a blind trust and is untouchable until the shareholders approve the acquisition transaction.

The SPAC goes public and trades on an exchange like any other publicly traded company.

This is where the general public gets involved. They can purchase securities on the open market, but the future acquisition is still unknown to them.

Instead, these investors are buying on the vision and the strength of the sponsor or the promise of a strong future acquisition.

Once the SPAC is public, the sponsors can begin the hunt for a target company to acquire.

This looks fairly simple on paper but is the journey from SPAC to i-SPAC all that same? Not all. However, to get a better idea of how complicated or simple going public is for a SPAC, I will dig deep into every step that is taken by it to become a public entity.

Why SPACs over Traditional IPO?

SPACs offer several benefits not provided by a conventional IPO to sponsor-organizers and businesses that choose to go public. One is the simplified criteria for disclosure that saves trees, funds, and time.

Another possible reason is that there have been instances in recent years of businesses taking the conventional IPO route and decreasing in value during the roadshow phase due to investor scrutiny, causing the company to withdraw its IPO filing.

By contrast, the SPAC IPO path entails relatively less investor scrutiny because the entity going public is not really a corporation, so there is not much to scrutinize.

This renders the SPAC IPO more appealing to riskier businesses or businesses in riskier sectors, such as the media industry.

This is particularly true if the current investors in those firms are anxious and looking for the business to sell or go public in order to cash out their shares.

Firms that are "risky enough" that they might not be accepted in the normal IPO market are those that are likely to opt for a SPAC IPO.

Are SPACs Free From Scrutiny in an IPO?

The nature of SPACs makes this an important question to answer. In a SPAC IPO, the scrutiny is not actually abolished. Instead, it is redirected and reduced.

The initial investors make the call of whether to take a gamble on the sponsor and acquisition strategy of the SPAC, knowing that if a majority disagrees with the ultimate acquisition target, they will have their money refunded.

Therefore, the acquisition could be more scrutinized by investors than the IPO. On the other hand, they (the investors) have already endorsed the sponsor championing the acquisition.

Therefore, the investors are likely to go along with the transaction unless the sponsor really goes off track with the acquisition target.

Does a SPAC IPO Involve the Same Number of People as a Traditional IPO?

The involvement of fewer individuals is another reason SPAC IPOs are so popular.

A conventional IPO involves many investors negotiating concurrently with issuers and underwriters on particular terms such as underwriter rights, executive pay, the offer price, and several other issues.

However, in a SPAC, it is generally just the target company and the sponsor that are involved in the negotiations. This helps to speed up the process.

Can SPAC Be Used By Company to Become Public?

This is a difficult one to answer. There seem to be no laws stopping a corporation from developing its own SPAC and then getting the SPAC to acquire it. However, this is not what happens in reality.

Rather, after the SPAC has gone public and the money for the purchase has been generated, the SPAC sponsor goes about seeking a business to acquire.

In addition, SPACs are not allowed to have a merger target in mind when they go public.

What Are the Incentives for SPAC Sponsors to Go Public Via SPAC?

One or more investment banks that earn an underwriting concession as an incentive to promote and sell the IPO can be underwriters of a conventional IPO.

The discount for conventional IPO underwriters is generally about 3.5-7 percent, as per PWC.

On the other hand, the SPAC IPO's underwriting concession is 5.5%, with 2% payment during the IPO and the remainder 3.5% payment at the time of the de-SPAC transaction.

In addition, the underwriting discount payment is usually made as equity options in the business to the SPAC sponsors.

The delayed discount commission helps the target organization and positively influences sponsors to identify a target acquisition to earn their 3.5 percent commission as equity.

To say it another way, instead of paying the SPAC sponsors in the form of equity, the payment that a corporation would make to an investment bank to underwrite an IPO is instead made to the SPAC sponsors.

Although the cost of going public could be more or less the same, in comparison to a conventional IPO, benefits for underwriters and the business are more integrated into the SPAC process.

Is SPAC IPO More Expensive Than Conventional IPO?

SPAC IPOs are typically more expensive than a conventional IPO. This is because you generally need to make payments to investment banks between 1 and 7% of what you generated to conduct an IPO.

The underwriter receives 5.5 percent in a SPAC and other expenses may be involved in the merger. For example, you must pay a bank to get advice on the deal.

So SPAC expenses are about a quarter of the funds collected - three or four times greater than what you would pay in an IPO. Additionally, in most instances, 20 percent of the stock is given 'on the cheap' to the sponsor.

How Does the SPAC IPO Process Work?

Initial business operations are financed by equity investment to initiate an initial public offering (IPO) and identify a planned acquisition. (Layne & Lenahan, 2018)

While the ratio may differ, about 20 percent of the post-offering stock is generally represented by the founders' stock.

The organization will put out an initial public offering (IPO) for investors soon after the SPAC is organized and will explain it in a prospectus.

This public offering enables SPAC to raise funds that will ultimately be used to acquire a target firm.

It is also necessary for a SPAC to become a publicly traded corporation so that when the businesses finally combine, the ultimate "target" can profit from that "public" status.

Units are usually the first security that is provided for selling as part of the SPAC IPO.

Not much later (typically 52 days), the units can be "split up" into their constituent elements to be traded as rights, warrants, and shares.

The SPAC IPO process generally works something like this. The SPAC files a statement of registration with the Securities and Exchange Commission (SEC) after choosing the underwriters in order to start the IPO.

After replying to the feedback of the SEC, the SPAC starts a roadshow resulting in the underwriting and IPO, the earnings of which are kept in a trust account awaiting an opportunity for investment.

Cash is generated by issuing warrants and common stock. A warrant is a security that gives the bearer of the warrant the right to purchase or sell a security.

Warrants are tradable and have a strike price at which, before expiry, the stock may be bought or sold.

At a price of $10, equity in a SPAC is sold as units consisting of a share plus a proportion of an out-of-the-money warrant.

For instance, a standard arrangement will be for the exercise to be $11.50 with a required conversion price considerably greater than that. In return for acquiring 20% of the units at a concession on the offering price, the sponsor will pump in money in the SPAC and cover costs.

The revenues from the SPAC capital increase are kept in a fiduciary account and can only be issued for one of three reasons:

(2) funding the purchase of the business; (2) to finance redemptions for shareholders; or (3) In the case of SPAC's liquidation, to pay investors if it is unable to conclude a deal within a defined timeframe (typically two years)

A shareholder also has an integrated put option, in addition to holding shares and warrants in a SPAC.

When an acquisition is declared, the investor has the option at the initial investment expense plus any accumulated interest to keep their stakes or to redeem their units.

This offers the investor many options to handle the position before the announcement of the agreement. They can choose to:

- Hold onto the entire unit (warrants and shares)
- When trading at a surplus to net asset value (NAV), sell the whole unit.
- Sell the shares but hold the warrants to benefit from a closed transaction from any possible upside

The sponsor will obtain no reward until a transaction is concluded with SPAC proceeds kept in trust.

The sponsor loses its capital investment if a target is not found and a transaction fails to materialize within the stated timeline, with residual profits credited to outside investors.

In this way, they are given incentives to ensure the completion of a deal and its alignment with external investors.

Is the Function of the SPAC Underwriter Same as the Underwriter of a Traditional IPO?

The underwriter of a SPAC IPO may have different functions concerning the SPAC (e.g., M&A financial advisor, private placement agent, and capital markets advisor).

Each potential new position should be scrutinized for conflicts of interest as an initial problem.

This is particularly important since the underwriter only retains a part of its underwriting concession (generally 35 basis points to be divided between the participants of the syndicate) if the SPAC performs an initial business combination.

Consequently, as the underwriter is engaged in any of the functions mentioned below, the underwriter should guarantee that the SPAC board of directors and, if applicable, investors are notified of this conflict of interest.

As the SPAC looks for and achieves its initial business combination goal, an underwriter of a SPAC IPO may be requested to aid in different activities related to capital markets.

This could include: (i) wall crossing accounts to engage in discussion regarding their views on a possible qualifying deal; (ii) scheduling accounts meetings before and during the period of proxy solicitation; (iii) facilitating the SPAC in preparing presentation materials.

The role that performs the activities listed above is often referred to as a "capital market advisor".

Supporting the SPAC in its investor relations poses possible problems under the rules of proxy solicitation.

It is also critical that the capital market advisor is not deemed to be a proxy applicant because the underwriter, operating as a capital market advisor, has failed to comply with the different rules and regulations related to proxy applicants (such as the rules found in Regulation 14A of the Exchange Act).

As a result, the underwriter working as an adviser on capital markets should consider restricting its operations to ministerial duties.

The underwriter should consider inserting language in these ministerial correspondences revealing that it stands to obtain its deferred compensation if the SPAC completes its original business combination.

The SPAC IPO's underwriter may be required to serve as a PIPE placement agent or to underwrite or organize debt financing.

Serving as a PIPE placement agent may be necessary to complete an original business combination in either case.

The underwriter should pursue its usual procedures for this form of participation, including, if necessary, heading into a separate letter of engagement, including a compensation agreement.

The letter of engagement should contain language revealing that if the SPAC completes its original business combination, the underwriter stands to receive the deferred compensation.

Using such terminology in materials submitted to investors should also be considered by the underwriter.

For a former SPAC IPO underwriter, it is normal to introduce future acquisition prospects to the SPAC.

This is where the previously serving underwriter either introduces the SPAC as the future prospect for acquisition or has the specific business experience to serve as a SPAC financial advisor.

If the former underwriter serves the SPAC in the capacity of an M&A in its original business combination, that underwriter must follow its usual practices for this type of intervention.

This involves entering into a different letter of engagement, including an indemnification deal, if necessary.

The letter of engagement should contain language revealing that if the SPAC completes its original business combination, the former underwriter stands to receive its deferred compensation.

The former underwriter may not want to give their viewpoint on fairness in relation to the original business combination, or the SPAC may not want them to do so.

This is because of the reporting of conflict of interest that would be needed in the viewpoint on fairness.

It is less usual for a former SPAC IPO underwriter to depict the target in an original business combination.

However, the fairness council of the underwriter may be satisfied promoting a target and even providing a fairness assessment (with the required conflict of interest reporting) based on the facts and situations.

This would probably be much more likely if the target is a private firm, and there is no need for publicly disclosing the fairness assessment of the target firm.

If the former underwriter serves the SPAC in its original business combination, then the former underwriter must follow its usual practices for this type of intervention.

This involves entering into a different letter of engagement, including an indemnification deal, if necessary.

The Discount Structure for SPAC IPO Underwriters

SPAC IPOs have a unique underwriting discount model. The underwriters usually earn a concession of 5%-7% of the gross IPO revenues in a conventional IPO, which they deduct from the revenues provided at closing.

The standard discount arrangement in a SPAC IPO is for 2% of the gross

revenues to be paid at the closing of the IPO, with another 3.5% being credited into the trust account and due to the underwriters at the close of the De-SPAC deal.

The deferred 3.5 percent discount is never provided to the underwriters if no De-SPAC transaction takes place and is used with the remainder of the trust account balance to reimburse the public shares.

A lock-up arrangement for 180 days from the pricing of the IPO is signed by the officers, directors, and sponsors in a conventional IPO.

The standard lock-up for a SPAC IPO lasts for up to one year from the closure of the De-SPAC deal, subject to early removal if the common shares are trading over a fixed price (typically $12.00 per share) for twenty out of thirty trading days beginning 150 days after the De-SPAC deal is completed.

Is The Insurance Capital Limited For SPAC IPOS?

For SPAC IPOs, there is limited insurance capital available. So, it's no wonder that costs are rising as demand grows.

Moreover, such a high degree of industry activity carries with it the potential for more lawsuits by shareholders.

D&O insurance carriers are worried because their money would be restricted if shareholders bring litigation alleging wrongful actions by the directors and officers of a SPAC.

Underwriters are also worried that the large amount of SPACs will encourage review of the Securities and Exchange Commission.

No applicant lawsuit against a SPAC IPO has been filed to date. As such, an accomplished insurance broker would be able to negotiate D&O coverage with significantly more favorable rates and SIRs than those of a traditional IPO scheme, even with rising costs.

That said, for SPAC IPOs, the D&O insurance marketplace is actually more restricted than for conventional operating firms.

For certain insurers, the blank-check nature is hard to model in their underwriting. There is confusion about where the trust's resources will be invested, and considering their re-insurance treaties, many carriers are reluctant to issue long-term policies.

Several factors make it difficult for certain carriers who can write D&O insurance for operating company IPOs to quote a SPAC policy. These include:

- On a multi-year basis, usually 24 months, a SPAC D&O policy is written to span the duration of the due diligence phase of the SPAC
- The program should include pre-agreed run-off or "tail" policy expenses and conditions to be effective when the market combination is closed. 'Tail' policies have an extended period of time, usually six years, to report claims for incidents that happened while the initial policy was in place. Preferably, any unearned premium should be repaid on a pro-rata basis if a de-SPAC transaction occurs before the end of the IPO agreement.

Of course, the fact that all D&O insurance companies do not offer these vital terms limits the insurance capital available for SPAC IPOs, another reason why premiums continue to increase.

What Factors are Considered When Underwriting SPAC IPOs for Insurance Purposes?

The following are some key considerations for underwriters when determining how much to charge for director and officers (D&O) insurance in a SPAC IPO.

THE BACKGROUND OF THE SPONSOR

The underwriters would reflect on the makeup of the board of directors and management team of the SPAC when evaluating the S-1.

The background, investing history and credibility of each member of the group in their particular industry and the SPAC field will be evaluated.

Compared to one comprised of less experienced members or those who have not engaged in a SPAC project before, a sponsor team made up of experienced SPAC veterans who have carried out numerous SPAC deals may be seen as a more appealing risk.

Moreover, insurance underwriters are suspicious about any SPAC officers or directors who may be noted for irregular conduct, and their services/interest would be priced accordingly.

EXPECTED FUNDRAISE AMOUNT

The bigger the fundraiser, the greater the premium for D&O policy and insured retention. Settlement sums in securities class action suits have traditionally been aligned with the market cap of a firm.

Thus, as an example, SPAC of $100 million would get quotes for D&O insurance with a lower premium and SIRs than a SPAC that is equal to or greater than $500 million.

TARGET CLASS OF BUSINESS FOR ACQUISITION AND ALIGNMENT WITH SPONSOR EXPERIENCE

Insurance underwriters would like to see a connection between the skills of the sponsor team and the identified category of potential businesses to acquire.

A board of individuals with a track history of investing in and running similar companies planning to do businesses in the same area would be treated favorably.

However, a team with relevant sector expertise that otherwise wants to invest resources in any other industry would be seen more negatively.

It should also be remembered that regardless of who is on the board, certain sectors are challenging; an example of this would be anything that has to do with cannabis.

TARGET BUSINESS GEOGRAPHY

D&O insurance carriers favor writing policies in regions and states where they know the laws of the state, corporate security laws and the landscape of the consumer economy.

Different insurers have stringent rules that stop them from covering regions where they do not have this knowledge and insight.

SPACs targeting companies in the United States, for instance, will find things less challenging with insurance underwriters than those trying to target companies in China.

In addition, certain domestic insurers can only write D&O policies for firms based in the United States.

SPECIFICITY OF THE TARGET CRITERIA PROVIDED IN THE S-1

The underwriters try to predict where the cash injection into the SPAC will ultimately be utilized in a transaction when reviewing the S-1

The more precise the details on the target business class and its location presented in the S-1 registration statement, the more confident the insurance underwriters are likely to be regarding the reliability of the information provided.

Therefore, underwriters would be more secure in their ability to interpret the reach of a SPAC's future acquisitions involving a "SaaS tech firm based in North America" as opposed to if the target description simply read "a tech firm without a worldwide location preference."

Being more precise about the target business class provides insurance underwriters with the ability to supply their rating system with extra credits.

FEDERAL FORUM PROVISIONS

D&O subscribers will request the incorporation of federal forum requirements in the corporate charter records of the SPAC.

An S-1 that specifically contains provisions of the federal forum would be deemed advantageous.

Insurance carriers will need assurance that the rules of the federal forum are shown in the charter documentation of the SPAC if it is not clear from the S-1.

If the provisions were not included in the charter papers, the underwriters would be less equipped to offer risk coverage.

POTENTIAL CONFLICTS OF INTEREST

When evaluating the SPAC profile, the insurance carriers would want to ensure that there are no conceivable potential conflicts in the relationships between the sponsors and the SPAC.

If the underwriters consider the "promote" or any other compensation earned by management to fund the SPAC to be too high, they would most likely hesitate to offer terms.

Additionally, the underwriters will evaluate the reporting of related party transactions.

For instance, carriers would like to avoid situations where sponsors buy a business where a director or officer has a previously defined connection to the target and would profit from the deal.

There would be less enthusiasm from the underwriters if there were any other provisions that could trigger doubt, such as an unusual warrant structure.

ADVISORY TEAM

Just like the history of the sponsor, the better the advisory team of the SPAC, the more confident the underwriters would be in writing the risk.

This group involves the external counsel of the SPAC, auditors, and investment bankers.

A SPAC would want to partner with reputable companies with a lot of experience in the comfort insurance business.

This is because these companies would have spent time and money to carry

out their own due diligence.

The SPAC is laying the groundwork for as effective an IPO launch as possible by seeking such assistance.

How Are SPAC IPO Shares Bought?

In its IPO, a SPAC usually issues units comprising of one share of stock and a portion of a warrant.

In general, SPAC non-affiliates can sell these units easily on the public market after the IPO.

The warrants and common stock will start selling separately shortly after the IPO and will continue being easily traded by non-affiliates.

Suppose the issuer does not complete a business merger within a certain permitted period of time (generally 18-24 months). In that case, the SPAC will reimburse the money in the trust account for any shares issued in its IPO and the warrants will expire meaninglessly.

Usually, the warrants will not be executed until 1 year after the IPO and thirty days after the business merger.

Although the SPAC shares are 'beneficially held' by investors until they are acquired for the reasons of Section 13(d), the warrants do not lead directly to the beneficial ownership of the underlying stock until the requirements for their exercise (i.e. company merger and registration) have been met.

As a SPAC investor, it is critical for you to understand how to determine your beneficial ownership.

This is important not only for the reasons of Section 13(d) reporting but also for recognizing the potential to cause Section 16 reporting and short-swing benefit disgorgement problems when you transact in the SPAC stocks.

What are The Most Important Things for SPAC IPO Investors to Know?

The following are some of the most important things for investors in SPAC IPO to know.

TRUST ACCOUNT

Usually, SPAC IPO revenues minus revenue used for some fees and costs are kept in a trust account.

A third party holds the money before the deal is finalized, equivalent to an escrow agreement when purchasing a property—in the case of a SPAC, the original business combination—or the SPAC is liquidated for not having concluded an initial business combination within a specified time period.

In general, SPACs invest the revenues in reasonably secure, interest-bearing investment vehicles.

However, the precise terms of the offer should be closely checked because there is no law requiring the revenues to be invested only in certain types of vehicles.

SPACs typically use the interest on trust account investments to pay taxes.

A SPAC gives its investors the ability to redeem their holdings connected with a corporate merger rather than simply being a shareholder in the merged entity.

If the SPAC does not complete a business merger, the investors shall be beneficiaries of the trust and shall have the right to their pro rata share of the net balance upon investment in the trust account.

One thing to remember is that you are only eligible for the pro rata share of the trust account if you bought the stock on the open market and not the rate at which you acquired the SPAC shares on the exchange.

For instance, if a SPAC conducted an IPO at $15 per share, but you acquired 100 SPAC shares at $16 per share on the open market, the stocks you buy are connected to a trust account balance of approximately $15 per share.

So your trust account share will be worth around $1500, rather than the $1600 you've paid for your stock.

To be clear about the conditions of the trust account, particularly your redemption privileges and the scenarios in which cash can be freed from the account, you should carefully read the SPAC IPO prospectus.

TRADING PRICE

Generally, SPACs are priced at a modest $10 per unit in the IPO. The SPAC IPO price is not dependent on the value of an established corporation, unlike the conventional IPO of an operating company.

When the warrants, common stock, and units start trading, their market values will fluctuate and there may be no connection between these variations and the SPAC's ultimate financial performance.

PERIOD TO FINALIZE THE ORIGINAL BUSINESS COMBINATION

A SPAC would usually allow for identifying and executing an initial business combination deal for a two-year duration. Some SPACs, however, have chosen shorter cycles, such as 18 months.

The governing instruments of the SPAC can allow the SPAC to prolong the duration.

If a SPAC wishes to extend the time span, investor approval will be needed.

If a SPAC lists its shares on a market, it is mandated to conclude an original business combination within three years of its IPO.

IPO revenues are kept in a trust account until a SPAC finalizes a business merger or liquidates.

If the SPAC liquidates, the owners will be eligible for their pro rata share of the net sum at the point of liquidation, then on investment in the trust account.

It is crucial to evaluate whether desirable initial business combinations will become elusive as the volume of SPACs wanting to acquire operating businesses increases.

WARRANTS

A SPAC IPO is often designed to sell a unit of securities to shareholders that comprise of (1) warrants and (2) common stock shares.

A warrant is an agreement that gives the holder the right to buy a specific number of extra common stock shares from the firm at a specific price in the future, often a premium to the existing stock price at the time of issuing the warrant.

For a while after the IPO, the SPAC unit will be traded. The warrants and common stocks of the SPAC may start trading on a market independently with their own unique trading labels sometime after the IPO.

The SPAC will usually file a current Form 8-K filing and release a statement informing investors when separate trading will begin.

Investors buying SPAC stocks on the open exchange after the IPO must know whether they are buying warrants, common stock, or units.

The conditions of warrants can vary considerably across various SPACs, and when investing, it is crucial to understand the conditions.

The conditions of the warrants may include the number of shares the holder is entitled to buy, the rate at which the stocks may be bought, and the period within which the stocks may be bought.

It may also include the conditions under which the warrants may be redeemed by the SPAC and the expiry of the warrants.

Investors should go through the IPO prospectus of the particular SPAC in order to understand more about the specific conditions.

REDEMPTION AND VOTE

Suppose a SPAC has established an initial business merger possibility. In that case, SPAC investors will have the chance to redeem their stock and, in many situations, vote on the initial business merger deal.

After the original business combination, each SPAC investor can either continue being a company shareholder or redeem and collect their pro rata sum of funds kept in the trust account.

As the SPAC transitions from simply a trust account into an operating entity, this is a vital investor factor.

As an investor, you can choose to redeem your stock for a pro rata share of the net sum on investment in the trust account or continue being an investor in the merged company going forward.

You can do the above based on how you see the potential initial business merger and its valuation.

PROXY, INFORMATION, OR TENDER OFFER STATEMENT

If SPAC requires shareholder acceptance of the initial business merger, a proxy statement will be given to investors in preparation for the shareholder vote.

In situations where the SPAC does not seek the consent of public shareholders since those investors, such as the sponsor and its associates, have ample votes to support the deal, the SPAC may provide investors with a declaration of facts prior to the conclusion of the initial business combination.

Relevant business details will be included in the proxy or knowledge statement.

This includes relevant details on the company's business, which the SPAC intends to acquire.

These details include the company's financial reports, the interests of the participants in the deal, such as the sponsor of the SPAC, and the conditions of the original business merger transaction, including the merged entity's capital structure.

If the deal is finalized and you decide that you do not wish to remain a shareholder, then you may do the following.

By completing the actions specified in the proxy or information statement, you can redeem your shares of common stock—first for your pro rata share of the net sum and then on investment into the trust account.

If a SPAC is not expected to send a proxy or information statement to investors (for instance, if a SPAC is not needed to acquire the transaction's shareholder approval), you will be provided with a tender offer statement containing information about the target company and your redemption rights.

The SEC's EDGAR database is where you can check the proxy, details or tender offer declaration of a SPAC.

THE SPONSOR'S INTEREST

In general, SPAC sponsors buy shares in SPAC on more advantageous terms than IPO investors or eventual free market investors.

Therefore, investors should be mindful that while IPO investors have given much of the SPAC's money, the sponsors and possibly other initial investors would benefit from the execution of an initial business combination by the

SPAC more than shareholders and will have an incentive to conclude a deal on conditions that may be less favorable to you.

In addition, additional funding may be needed by the SPAC to finance the original business combination, and such funding often includes sponsors.

As a consequence, the sponsors' interests could deviate further from your interests.

For instance, additional sponsor support may diminish your interest in the merged entity or it may be given in the form of a loan or protection that has rights different from your investments.

You should examine the "Principal Stockholders" and "Certain Relationships and Related Party Dealings" parts of the IPO prospectus of a SPAC to know more about the objectives of a sponsor in a SPAC.

From the tender offer statement, information statement, or proxy statement, you can know more about an initial business merger and the sponsor's involvement in it.

What Are the Critical Laws That SPAC IPOs Must Adhere To?

The following are some securities laws for SPAC IPOs that must be considered prior to taking a SPAC public via an IPO. (Overy, 2020)

Exemption from "Blank-Check Company" Status under Rule 419

SPACs are intended to avoid being listed under the securities laws as "blank-check companies".

This is because, under Rule 419 of the Securities Act of 1933, as modified (the 'Securities Act'), a blank-check company must, among other things, deposit into an escrow account all revenues and securities provided in its IPO.

In addition, there is a ban on transferring or exchanging securities before a business combination has been completed.

While it has become the market standard for SPACs to deposit funds into an escrow account, it would be an obstacle to limiting trading before a business combination is completed.

The paperwork for most SPACs typically requires up to 24 months for the SPAC to complete this process.

The issuer must offer "penny stock," as specified in Rule 3a51-1 under the Securities Exchange Act of 1934, as modified (the "Exchange Act"), to be considered a blank-check company.

Exchange Act Rule 3a51-1(g) excludes any protection of an issuer that has been in service for less than three years and has a minimum of $5 million in net tangible assets from the scope of penny stock.

To be able to profit from this restriction, the SEC needs the issuer to file Form 8-K with a verified balance sheet as soon as possible after the IPO to show compliance.

SPACs usually use the exclusion of Exchange Act Rule 3a51-1(g) and escape the requirements under Rule 419.

Usually, the IPO registration declaration of a SPAC would state that the SPAC will submit such a Form 8-K immediately after the IPO is consummated.

If an overallotment option is exercised after the submission of this Form 8-K, a separate Form 8-K with a revised audited balance sheet showing the overallotment exercise would need to be submitted by the SPAC.

Usually, the underwriting agreement also includes covenants that enable the SPAC to submit Form 8-K.

SPACs as Shell Companies and Ineligible Issuers

A SPAC is deemed a "shell company" under Securities Act Rule 4055 even though it is excluded from Securities Rule 419. As such, the following applies to it:

- A SPAC is an "unqualified issuer," as specified in Securities Act Rule 405, and therefore may not use prospectuses for free writing (the roadshow presentations are subject to additional limitations without the use of the free writing prospectus guidelines).
- SPAC securities owners may not depend on Securities Act Rule 144 for the resale of such securities until one year after completion of the SPAC's initial business combination and submission of current Form 10 details to the SPAC (the SPAC must also have submitted the periodic reports needed under Section 13 or Section 15(d) of the Exchange Act (besides the Form 8-K) for the preceding twelve months (or for such a shorter time as to enable the SPAC to submit such reports).
- Until three years have passed since its initial business combination, a SPAC will not become a well-known experienced issuer; and
- Many of the correspondence safe harbors under the Securities Act cannot be used by a SPAC.

INVESTMENT COMPANY ACT

The arrangement of the trust account of a SPAC is structured to prevent the SPAC from being listed under the Investment Company Act of 1940, as modified (the "Investment Company Act"), as an "investment company."

A SPAC is usually expected, following its IP, to allocate the IPO revenues held in trust in either government securities or money market funds that only invest in government securities.

In doing so, under the Investment Company Act, a SPAC can depend on Rule 3a-1. This prohibits firms with no more than 45 percent of the value of their total assets comprising securities and no more than 45 percent of the issuer's net income after tax derived from securities (not including government securities).

There are also no-action letters in which SEC personnel accept that securities can also be exempt from these estimates in some money market funds.

EMERGING GROWTH COMPANY

A SPAC, as described in Section 2(a)(19) of the Securities Act, may be deemed an Emerging Growth Company ('EGC') and, if so, will stay an EGC until earlier than :

iii. On the last day of the financial year (a) following the fifth anniversary of the conclusion of the IPO, (b) the cumulative gross annual revenue of the SPAC is minimum $1.07 billion per year (updated every five years for inflation), or (c) where the market value of its common equity owned by non-affiliates as of before 30 June crosses $700 million (or the end of the second financial quarter, if not a business ending December 31 financial year); and

iv. The date on which more than $1 billion of non-convertible debt securities were issued by SPAC over the previous three-year period.

If SPAC (newly deSPAC-ed) continues to be considered as an EGC under these rules after its initial business combination, the firm will continue to benefit from that status.

How Can Warrants Be Exercised by SPAC IPO Investors and Is There a Time Limit for It?

Investors who take part in the SPAC IPO are drawn by the ability to exercise the warrants so that, once the purchase target is determined and the deal concludes, they can get more common stock shares.

The selling price of the shares per unit is normally $10.00. After the IPO, the units are divided into common stock shares and warrants that can be sold publicly

The intent behind the warrant is to provide extra compensation to shareholders for making investments in SPAC.

One warrant may be excised for a portion of a share (either half, one-third or two-thirds) or a whole share of the stock, depending on the SPAC's size and the bank issuing the IPO.

For instance, the warrant could be exercisable at $16.50 per share if the unit price in the IPO is $15.

The warrants become exercisable either thirty days after the De-SPAC transaction or an entire year following the SPAC IPO.

Sponsor/founder warrants and public warrants (i.e., unit warrants) have exactly the same conditions and cannot be exercised till the business combination agreement with an operating entity has been completed.

The public warrants are cash-settled, which ensures that to obtain a full share of stock, the investor would have to pay the full price of the warrant in cash.

On the other hand, Founder warrants could be net settled, which ensures that they are not expected to offer cash to obtain a full share of stock

Instead, stock shares with a fair market value proportional to the difference between the stock exchange price and the strike price of a warrant are issued to them.

The conditions of warrants can vary considerably across various SPACs, and when investing, it is crucial to understand the conditions.

The conditions of the warrants may include the number of shares the holder is entitled to buy, the rate at which the stocks may be bought, and the period within which the stocks may be bought.

It may also include the conditions under which the warrants may be redeemed by the SPAC and the expiry of the warrants.

Warrants are provided to institutional investors to exercise as incentives for investing pre-IPO.

Usually, the warrants will not be executed until 1 year after the IPO and thirty days after the business merger.

Although the SPAC shares are 'beneficially held' by investors until they are acquired for the reasons of Section 13(d), the warrants do not lead directly to the beneficial ownership of the underlying stock until the requirements for their exercise (i.e. company merger and registration) have been met.

All the rights/warrants/shares are directly transferred to the related rights/warrants/shares/units of the newly established firm when the transaction eventually concludes.

If the stock of the new business increases for a specific number of days beyond a certain level (the exact price is specified in the prospectus but is typically $18), the firm may leverage the warrants to be redeemed.

That implies that a particular date is presented to warrant holders before which they have to take one of the following actions.

They either have to utilize their warrants (i.e., change them to shares) or trade them. Otherwise, the warrants become useless.

When Does the Warrant Expire?

The expiry date of warrants is five years from the time of the De-SPAC. After this time, the warrants become useless and the initial warranties will no longer liquidate the target firm's stock.

This concludes the discussion on how SPACs can go public via an IPO.

NEW YORK STOCK EXCHANGE
ONE WAY
WALL ST
NEW ST

Conclusion

In 2020, 247 newly created SPACs generated $83 billion in capital via initial public offerings. More SPACs were established in 2019 and 2020 than in the previous 18 years together.

Not only is the quantity of SPACs growing, but each SPAC raises enough capital via IPOs to be able to buy larger private firms.

The typical IPO process is turned on its head by a SPAC in that the business that originally goes public is not so much a corporation as the expectation of one. In other words, the SPAC is just a shell company that does not own any assets itself.

A SPAC can be seen as the opposite of a conventional IPO. A SPAC first goes public, typically with a highly respected management team capable of raising capital from large institutional investors, with the goal of purchasing a private firm within around 24 months to place it in its shell.

An IPO is essentially a money-seeking business, whereas a SPAC is a business seeking money. Going public via a SPAC will speed up the market entry of a business by anywhere from two to four months.

SPACs offer several benefits not provided by a conventional IPO to sponsor-organizers and businesses that choose to go public. One is the simplified criteria for disclosure that saves trees, funds, and time.

Another possible reason is that, in recent years, there have been instances of businesses taking the conventional IPO route and decreasing in value during the roadshow phase due to investor scrutiny, causing the company to withdraw its IPO filing.

By contrast, the SPAC IPO path entails relatively less investor scrutiny because the entity going public is not really a corporation, so there is not much to scrutinize.

This renders the SPAC IPO more appealing to riskier businesses or businesses in riskier sectors, such as the media industry.

Considering the lack of financial reports and related materials, there are fewer SEC concerns and queries to answer without a corporation in the actual shell, which shortens the auditing process.

Additionally, instead of attempting to sell a business to public investors at a roadshow, a SPAC provides added assurity of getting a long-term investor base through a private-public equity fund, or PIPE, that is in place.

Usually, that kind of assurance is not available in an IPO unless it is perfectly clear that the business will do well.

SPACs today offer an effective alternative to the conventional IPO and a viable alternative to private equity firms that usually search for an exit after a couple of years.

As discussed in this book, there are many advantages of going public via a SPAC. The book makes it easier for you to decide whether to go public via a SPAC or not by discussing the advantages, disadvantages, key players, process, lifecycle, timeline, and legal structure of a SPAC.

The book also helps you distinguish between a shell and a SPAC and illustrates the key benefits that SPAC IPO has over the traditional initial public offering (IPO) process.

Hopefully, this information will be enough to help you to make the right decision regarding going public via a SPAC.

Bibliography

Abrahamson, M., Jenkinson, T., & Jones, H. (2011). Why don't US issuers demand European fees. *The Journal of Finance.*

Aggarwal, R. (2000). Stabilization activities by underwriters after initial public offerings. *The Journal of Finance.*

Boyer, C., & Baigent, G. (2008). "SPACs as alternative investments",. *The Journal of Private.*

Carpentier, C., Cumming, D., & Suret, J.-M. (2012). The Value of Capital Market Regulation:. *Journal of Empirical Legal Studies.*

Chemmanur, T. J., & Fulghieri, P. (1997). Why include warrants in new equity issues? A theory of Unit IPOs. *Journal of Financial and Quantitative Analysis.*

Chen, H. C., & Ritter, J. R. (2000). The seven percent solution. *The Journal of Finance.*

Cumming, D., Haß, L. H., & Schweizer, D. (2014). The Fast Track IPO–Success Factors for Taking Firms Public With SPACs. *Journal of Banking and Finance.*

Daks, M. (2020). *A SPAC is a high-risk but potentially profitable way to get in on the ground floor of a new stock – here's everything investors need to know.* Retrieved from Business Insider: https://www.businessinsider.com/what-is-a-spac

Dimitrova, L. (2017). "Perverse incentives of special purpose acquisition companies, the "poor. *Journal of Accounting & Economics.*

Eavis, P., & Meced, M. (2019, September). *WeWork I.P.O. Is Withdrawn as Investors Grow Wary.* Retrieved from The New York Times: https://www.nytimes.com/2019/09/30/business/wework-ipo.html

Hanley, K. W., & Hoberg, G. (2010). The Information Content of IPO Prospectuses. *Review of Financial Studies.*

Harroch, R., Raman, H., & Vanderlaan, A. (2020, November). *10 Key Questions And Answers About SPACs.* Retrieved from Forbes: https://www.forbes.com/sites/allbusiness/2020/11/11/10-key-questions-and-answers-about-spacs/?sh=67527de82f83

Heyman, D. K. (2007). From Blank Check to SPAC: The Regulator's Response to the Market, and. *Entrepreneurial Business Law Journal.*

Howe, J. S., & O'Brien, S. W. (2012). SPAC Performance, Ownership and Corporate Governance. *Advances in Financial Economics.*

Insider, S. (2020). *SPAC Statistics* . Retrieved from SPAC Insider: https://spacinsider.com/stats/?utm_source=markets&utm_medium=ingest

Investopedia. (2020). *https://www.investopedia.com/terms/s/spac.asp.* Retrieved January 20, 2021, from https://www.investopedia.com/terms/s/spac.asp

Jenkinson, T., & Sousa, M. (2011). Why SPAC Investors Should Listen to the Market (. *Journal of Applied Finance.*

Jog, V., & Sun, C. (2007). Blank Check IPOs: A Home Run for Management.

Kenton, W. (2020). *Shell Corporation.* Retrieved from Investopedia: https://www.investopedia.com/terms/s/shellcorporation.asp

Kolb, J., & Tykvová, T. (2016). Going public via special purpose acquisition companies: Frogs do. *Journal of Corporate Finance.*

Lakicevic, M., & Vulanovic, M. (n.d.). A Story on SPACs. Managerial Finance. *2013*, 384-403.

Layne, R., & Lenahan, B. (2018, July 6). *Special Purpose Acquisition Companies: An Introduction.* Retrieved from Harrvard Law School Forum on Corporate Governance: https://corpgov.law.harvard.edu/2018/07/06/special-purpose-acquisition-companies-an-introduction/

Levine, M. (2020, July 27). *SPACs Aren't Cheaper Than IPOs Yet.* Retrieved from Bloomberg: https://www.bloomberg.com/opinion/articles/2020-07-27/spacs-aren-t-cheaper-than-ipos-yet

Mitchell, M., & Pulvino, T. (2012). Arbitrage crashes and the speed of capital. *Journal of Financial Economics .*

Murray, J. S. (2014). The Regulation and Pricing of Special Purpose Acquisition Corporation IPOs.

Overy, A. &. (2020). *The Journey to De-SPACing and Beyond; Key securities laws considerations for former SPACs.* Allen & Overy.

pwc. (n.d.). *Considering an IPO? First, understand the costs.* Retrieved from pwc.com: https://www.pwc.com/us/en/services/deals/library/cost-of-an-ipo.html

pwc Price Waterhouse Cooper. (2017). *How special purpose acquisition companies (SPACs) work.* Retrieved January 20, 2021, from https://www.pwc.com/us/en/services/audit-assurance/accounting-advisory/spac-merger.html#:~:text=A%20SPAC%20raises%20capital%20through,of%20executing%20its%20own%20IPO.

Rodrigues, U., & Stegemoller, M. (2014). What all-cash companies tell us about IPOs and. *Journal of Corporate Finance,* 111-121.

Rodrigues, U., & Stegemoller, M. (2014). What all-cash companies tell us about IPOs and aquistions. *Journal of Corporate Finance.*

SEC. (2020). NOTE 1. DESCRIPTION OF ORGANIZATION AND BUSINESS OPERATIONS.

Wikipedia. (2020). *Special-purpose_acquisition_company*. Retrieved January 20, 2021, from https://en.wikipedia.org/wiki/Special-purpose_acquisition_company

Yochanan, S., & Milos, V. (2018). SPAC IPOs. *Oxford Handbook of IPOs*.